BARBECUE

UNBEATABLE RECIPES, TIPS & TRICKS FROM A BARBECUE CHAMPION

~SECRETS~

BARBECUE

UNBEATABLE RECIPES, TIPS & TRICKS FROM A BARBECUE CHAMPION

~SECRETS~

Ron Shewchuk

whitecap

⌐ To the Butt Shredders ⌐

Edited by Elaine Jones
Proofread by Marial Shea
Cover and interior design by Jacqui Thomas
Food photographs by John Sinal
Food styling by Joanne Facchin
Some photographs courtesy of the Brinkman Corporation and Modern Home Products, Corporation
Additional photography by Rick McCharles, Ian Baird, Peter Findlay and Vince Gogolek
Visit Ron Shewchuk's website at www.ronshewchuk.com

Printed and bound in Canada

NATIONAL LIBRARY OF CANADA CATALOGUING IN PUBLICATION

Shewchuk, Ron
    Barbecue secrets: unbeatable recipes, tips and tricks from a barbecue champion / Ron Shewchuk.

Includes index.
ISBN 1-55285-523-6

    1. Barbecue cookery. I. Title.
TX840.B3S55 2004   641.5'784   C2004-900371-2

The publisher acknowledges the financial support of the Government of Canada through the Book Publishing Industry Development Program for our publishing activities.

CONTENTS

FOREWORD

Step away from this cookbook. You're only going to get yourself in trouble.

Finger-lickin', lip-smackin' trouble. The kind of trouble that goes with those sultry summer days that liquefy into long, hot nights. The kind of trouble that puts a smile on your lips...and meat on your hips. Yeah, that kind.

So step away. There's nothing to see here ...unless you happen to be a devotee of great grilled or barbecued food. Not just a devotee, but a kind of pilgrim on a quest for the best. This is a pilgrim's manual. This will set you on the path to barbecue righteousness. Say amen, somebody.

Rockin' Ronnie Shewchuk, a carnivore's carnivore, has been grilling since he was a teenager in Alberta, Canada. But it was about a dozen years ago that Rockin' (as he is known by his friends) discovered Southern-style barbecue—barbecue the noun, not the verb. Fatty meats, smoked long and slow over low wood and charcoal heat, produce a melt-in-your-mouth goodness that enchanted Rockin' from the start. Soon afterward, he and a group of fellow enthusiasts formed their competitive barbecue team, Rockin' Ronnie's Butt Shredders, and began hauling in the ribbons and trophies at contests throughout western Canada and the U.S.

Pieces of barbecue equipment began to accumulate in the backyard like Tribbles once did in Star Trek's Enterprise. Charcoal smoke would billow out of them most weekends through the summer. You couldn't pry the guy away from the smoker unless it was to get him to grill a little something.

Yet there were few complaints.

Rockin' would fire up his portable barbecue at the beach and find himself doling out samples to strangers who were salivating over the scent of his lamb burgers. The Butt Shredders would pull a glistening brisket off the rack after its 18-hour sauna at a competition and have line-ups of willing guinea pigs, ready to taste a sample-sized portion of barbecue heaven. Already a working journalist, I suddenly found myself reporting on Rockin's barbecue career.

Barbecue soon became a way of life. Family vacations were wedged in around competitions in Alberta, British Columbia, Oregon, Tennessee and Missouri. Dinner guests started looking disappointed when they heard Rockin' was not the one cooking that night. After he scooped up first prize for best burger in Canada at the Canadian National Barbecue Competition in Whistler, B.C., Rockin's kids' friends began telling them, "I hear your dad makes the best burgers. Can he cook one for me?"

Is this the sort of scenario you would like to see replayed in your own home? Wipe that goofy glazed look off your face, now, and answer me. Is it?

That's what I mean. Step away from this cookbook. You're only going to get yourself in trouble.

Don't say you weren't warned.

Kate Zimmerman
Barbecue Widow

P.S. Family motto? Live fast, die young and leave a well-marbled corpse.

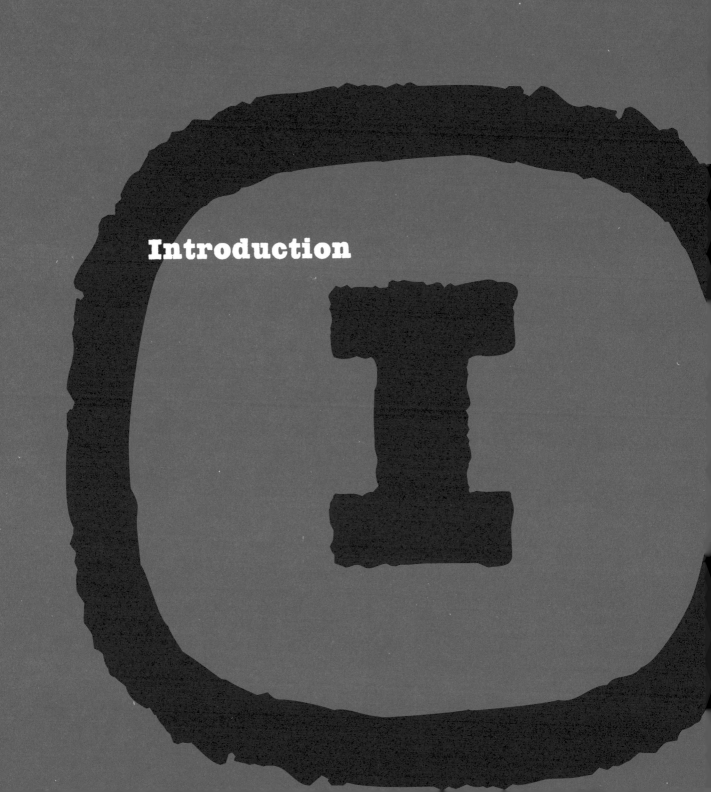

Introduction

Since our ancestors first learned that meat tastes better when it's held over a flame for awhile, we have been in love with outdoor cooking. It's one of the reasons we look forward to summer; it's a deep source of personal fulfilment and pride for husbands and dads everywhere; and for some of us, myself included, it's a lifestyle.

In fact, I would say barbecue is even more than a lifestyle. It's a philosophy that says barbecue, not the sun, is the center of the known universe, and that most important things in life rotate around (or in) that grill in your backyard. Things like friendship, family, good humor, tall tales and delicious food and drink.

Ever since I was a little boy I've been fascinated with meat. One of my first memories of great food is seeing my dad throw a big juicy sirloin steak in a cast iron frying pan on the wood-burning cookstove of our cottage. I remember the sharp hiss as the meat hit the pan, the sizzle as it cooked in a hot pool of butter, and, more than anything, the incredible smell of the searing black pepper working in perfect harmony with the rich aroma of the beef itself.

And the taste of it! Dad saw me standing by the stove and, when the steak was almost ready, he cut a little corner off it right in the pan and offered it to me at the end of a fork. That first taste—the fat, salty, peppery, juicy, crispy, chewy corner of a perfectly cooked steak—is a sensation that I chase every time I grill a piece of meat. And, like the first ice-cold gulp of a freshly cracked can of beer on a hot day, it's an elusive feeling, an ideal that's hard for most of us to attain.

I can offer a little help in this regard. After a lifetime as a backyard cook and a meat lover, and nearly a decade of pursuing my passion for traditional, Southern-style barbecue on the competitive barbecue circuit, I am throwing open the doors to the *sanctum sanctorum* of championship barbecue and sharing my barbecue secrets with you.

You may not want to live in a world where crazed, obsessive competitors tend a piece of meat over a slow hardwood fire for up to 24 hours—a world in which half-drunk debates can rage about whether you should put your brisket on the grill with the fat side down or up. The goal of this cookbook is to give you the tips, techniques and recipes to produce championship-quality meals on your grill or smoker so that you become the barbecue champion of your family, your friends, and your neighborhood. I also want to give you a little taste of the history and traditions of North American barbecue culture, which is stronger than ever and growing by leaps and bounds.

Throughout this book you will learn the secrets of championship barbecue—the tools and techniques that the pit masters use to win on the barbecue circuit. The biggest secret of championship barbecue is that there is no one secret, but rather a few basic principles and a lot of little things you can do to improve the quality of what you're grilling or barbecuing. Underlying this, though, is something successful barbecue cooks all have in common, and that's a true passion for this style of cooking. If this book can get you as excited about grilling and barbecue as I am, you're on your way to a special, smokey kind of glory.

There are scores of barbecue books out there, many of them written by true superstars of barbecue, who have cooked more meat and won more trophies than I could hope to achieve in five lifetimes. What I hope to bring to you and your table is the perspective of a born-again barbecuer—someone who is totally thrilled by his journey into the world of barbecue and passionately wants to share what he has learned along the way.

Rockin' Ronnie

P.S. Find me at www.ronshewchuk.com

THE ORIGINS OF BARBECUE

"The story of barbecue is the story of America: Settlers arrive on great unspoiled continent, discover wondrous riches, set them on fire and eat them."

— VINCE STATEN

Who the heck knows when the first primitive human being put the first chunk of meat near a fire? It was thousands of years before humans had the capacity to drink beer and use a basting brush, but that's all we know for sure.

What we do know is the first record of American barbecue was documented by Spanish conquistadors in the early 16th century. In between plunderings, the Spaniards noted that the Arawak aboriginal people of the Carribean used a raised platform called a *barbaca* made of green wood to cook meat above a smoldering fire. Some historians note that the Arawak also used the grill to roast their enemies. The word evolved into the Spanish *barbacòa*, a term still in use today in that language. Over time, *barbacòa* became Americanized, tansforming into the term we all know and love.

That's not the only theory. There's also the origin of the word that is consistently discounted or thrown out altogether by American barbecue pundits, but which I think is not bad at all. Apparently in France, when a butcher or a chef skewers a whole animal for cooking over a fire, he does it from beard to tail, or *de barbe à queue*...hence barbecue. This kind of term could easily have migrated into Southern Creole dialects and then moved into American English. But, in a continuation of the long-standing cultural and political feud between the United States and France, Americans scoff at this theory. Famed barbecue scholar and historian Smokey Hale discounts the French origin in classic barbecue style: "The French claim...is flagrantly fatuous franco-poop," writes Hale, a Texan, in an essay on the origins of barbecue. "If Catherine de Medici had not sent for her [Italian] chefs when she became queen of France, the French would probably still be groveling for gruel." Go, Smokey, go!

Cut to the U.S. southeast coast, where the aboriginal practice of cooking meat on a *barbacòa*-style contraption was observed by Spanish explorer deSoto's crewmen in the 1600s. One account describes a group of natives roasting venison and turkeys on a *barbacòa* near the Ocmulgee River, which is in present-day Georgia. This was a profoundly historic moment: the first recorded tailgate party in North America.

Meanwhile, on the west coast, people had been catching salmon and cooking it over smokey fires for about 8,000 years. Their technique was to skewer a big slab of freshly caught salmon on a stick and jab it into the ground close to a hot alder or cedar fire, which infused it with a lovely aroma and helped preserve the meat. They

Grilling vs. Barbecue

Before we get on with anything else I want to make an important distinction between grilling and barbecue. When most North Americans, particularly those north of the Mason-Dixon line, think about "barbecuing" or "having a barbecue," they mean grilling. That is, searing a seasoned steak or some marinated chicken for a few minutes on a propane, natural gas or charcoal grill. The grill makes nice marks on the meat, the drippings and ensuing flare-ups create a distinctive charred taste, and the high heat makes for convenient, quick and tasty cooking.

But it ain't barbecue. For die-hard barbecue fanatics, grilling is the culinary equivalent of bait-fishing—as viewed by those who find fly-casting the only true and pure form of angling. (They're the ones who derisively refer to bait fishermen as "worm drowners.")

For the purist, barbecue is not a convenient way of cooking—a 15-minute pre-dinner activity. Rather, it's something you eat at a roadside barbecue joint, or you cook yourself, for a long time, in a specialized piece of equipment called a smoker or barbecue pit. Traditional, Southern-style barbecue, or "Q" as it's sometimes called, consists of big, tough, fatty cuts of meat like pork shoulders and beef briskets that are cooked for many hours in a closed chamber, immersed in the vapors produced by a smoldering charcoal or hardwood fire. It's this style of cooking that is the basis of the growing number of barbecue competitions across the continent. There are even several governing bodies of barbecue, including the Kansas City Barbecue Society (KCBS), which lay down strict rules and judging criteria for barbecue competitions. And, like pro boxing, there are several huge contests that claim to be the world championship of barbecue. But we'll get to that later.

In this book I will be making the distinction between grilling and traditional barbecue, but I will give equal treatment to each. When I say grilling, it means what you do on your propane or charcoal grill. When I refer to barbecue, or barbecuing, it means the traditional, "low and slow" style of cooking that is one of the few truly indigenous American styles of cooking. For me, both techniques are great ways to achieve a fulfilling meat-eating experience. In fact, many of the tricks and recipes used in competitive barbecue can be easily adapted for use by the home cook.

So, throughout this book you will see phrasing that might seem awkward at first, like, "The single most important factor in cooking great barbecue is the rub," or "I love barbecue." Get used to it. After you've read and digested this book I expect you to become a barbecue ambassador in your community. If you truly love barbecue, you have to speak it, too!

didn't call it barbecue, but that's certainly what it was.

But back to the east coast. It wasn't long before the American settlers, upon observing the natives' *barbacòa* cooking technique, would apply it to the descendants of the pigs who came over with the first European settlers. As the eastern states became populated with European settlers and the rich bounty of North America began to reward those who took the risk of settling there, the pig became an integral part of the early American lifestyle. Hogs were plentiful and easy to raise, but refrigeration did not exist, and salt was at a premium. If you don't have salt or a fridge, the next best preservatives are sugar and vinegar. And, in a fruit-deprived, scurvy-prone society, a big source of vitamin C was the chili pepper.

And so it came to pass that whole hogs were smoked over hardwood fires and mopped with a mixture of vinegar, sugar and chilis. It was the perfect staple food for the pioneers, and this style of cooking is how barbecue is still practised in the eastern states to this day.

This take on the history of barbecue happens to be consistent with another tale relating to the origin of the word "barbecue". A wealthy South Carolina rancher named Bernard Quayle was in the habit of throwing huge outdoor feasts for hundreds of guests featuring pit-roasted sheep, hogs and steers. The story goes that the name of his ranch (also his cattle brand) was B̄Q̄, or Bar-B-Q. The name, over time, became associated with his style of entertaining and the term barbecue was born. Although this is an unlikely theory for the origin of the word barbecue, I like to think that old Mr. Quayle had a sense of humor. Seeing the similarity between his initials and what he liked to serve his guests, he turned his cattle brand into a visual pun. Although the word may not have been originated by him, the spirit of fun that we associate with barbecue may have had its beginnings with this Q-loving rancher.

If we see the east coast of the United States as the point of entry for barbecue, it's not too hard to document its migration west. From the Carolinas and Georgia to Tennessee, to Missouri and on to the great state of Texas, barbecue spread across America, with each region adding its own distinctive style. Memphis pretty much kept with the whole hog tradition of the east coast. Kansas City perfected pork ribs and added the thick, sweet, tangy, tomatoey sauce that most people today associate with barbecue. And Texas ... well, as we all know, it's a whole other country. And Texas is beef country, where big briskets are cooked "low and slow" and barbecue's roots go real deep.

To get at how we arrived at the classic American barbecue of today, the trail leads from the U.S. east coast down to Texas in the 1800s, where settlers used open pits to cook game such as squirrels and venison. Then, a major turning point in barbecue history: along came a wave of European immigrants in the last half of the 1800s, including German and Czech butchers, who had their own barbecue tradition.

How do you run a butcher shop and sell meat in hot old Texas with no refrigeration? The answer is simple: sell as much fresh meat as you can, and then smoke the leftovers (including sausages and tougher cuts of meat) in a big brick wood-fired oven, the precursor of the modern barbecue pit.

There was a growing market for this delicious leftover meat. Cotton farmers from all over the south flooded into Texas in the 1850s to buy cheap land, and with them came thousands of African-American slaves who were freed in 1865. These folks may have been free, but at the time there were few restaurants in that part of the world that would serve them after a long day of picking cotton. But the meat markets would. They sold hunks of smoked meat on a sheet of butcher paper to the hungry farm workers, who would enjoy it sitting on a nearby curb. There are still some barbecue joints—and butcher shops—in Texas that serve barbecue exactly the same way to this day.

The rise of German-style meat markets and barbecue restaurants represents an important branch of the history of barbecue. Another key ingredient in the historical mix is the tradition of giant parties hosted by politicians to attract a crowd leading up to election time—and to reward the faithful once they got into power. American president Lyndon Baines Johnson hosted many a barbecue on his sprawling Texas ranch and first lady Lady Bird would hand out recipe cards for her buttery barbecue sauce to constituents who wrote her at the White House.

THE GOLDEN AGE OF BARBECUING AND GRILLING

Today everyone in the American South has a personal vision of the best barbecue, generally associated with their favorite roadside barbecue joint, with its Formica-top tables, dingy lighting and charmingly grumpy servers. But what of barbecue and the home cook? How did we get to the point where we are today, with almost everyone in North America owning some kind of a backyard cooking device, and the growth of barbecue contests across the continent?

The history of backyard barbecuing and grilling goes back to the good old oil drum, which, when cut in half lengthwise, hinged, and stood up on metal legs, lifts the traditional barbacòa fire off the ground to create the prototypical modern barbecue pit. The halved oil drum was the device of choice of working class Americans, black and white, who learned to turn the fattiest, cheapest cuts of meat into barbecue heaven. It didn't matter who you were, or where you were. In post-war America, especially in the South, you got to smell and taste this indigenous cooking. Pork shoulders and ribs, beef brisket, hot links (fatty beef sausage), mutton and chicken, it all became fodder for amateur pit masters.

At that time we saw a split between grilling and barbecue, the two classic styles of backyard cooking. An open half drum, with

The First ⇜ Barbecue Joint? ⇝

By the 1850s a flood of German immigrants had created the Texas "German belt" of farm communities stretching into the hills outside of Houston and people of German descent made up about five percent of the total population of Texas. Kreuz Market was founded at the turn of the century in Lockhart, Texas, and featured a large brick oven at the back of the store with a firebox on one side and a chimney on the other. Sausages and leftover cuts of beef and pork were smoked according to European tradition, unsauced and seasoned simply with salt and pepper. The meat was sold over the counter on sheets of butcher paper, with no forks, knives or condiments other than the pickles and crackers sold in the shop. Kreuz Market is one of Texas's best-known purveyors of barbecue to this day, and although it moved to a bigger location in 1999, it is still a butcher shop selling barbecue on sheets of butcher paper, same way as always, with pickles and crackers.

The History of the ⇒ Backyard Grill ⇐

Before the rise of covered grilling in the 1950s, the classic home barbecue was more like a brazier—usually a square or round sheet metal contraption, perhaps with a cowling to hold a rotisserie and a compartment above for keeping side dishes warm, but mainly it was a rectangular box, or a bowl-shaped device in which you placed charcoal, with a removable grate on top to put your meat. I remember the one we had out at our family cottage had a grill that was fixed on a giant screw. To raise or lower the grill, you had to screw or unscrew it from its base. I still remember the squeaky sound the screw made, and the way Dad rolled around in the grass screaming that time he tried to light the coals with gasoline and burned himself. Good times.

The era of modern grilling was born when, in 1951, a welder from Chicago named George Stephen got so frustrated with using his open grill in the Windy City that he decided to do something about it. George worked at Weber Brothers Metal Works welding together large round metal buoys for the Coast Guard. Working with the buoys all day inspired George to build a cooker with the same materials—a bowl-shaped device with a lid, an air vent and three spindly metal legs that would become the prototype of the Weber Kettle, which in some circles is as recognizable an icon today as the Coke bottle.

Perhaps even more recognizable today is the omnipresent outdoor gas grill, which was invented by Walter Koziol, founder of Modern Home Products in

charcoal or hardwood coals directly underneath a grate, is essentially a brazier or grill, designed to sear meat and cook food relatively quickly. But cover that device with the other half of the barrel and you have a closed chamber. Push the fire to one side, keep the heat low, put a pan of water underneath the meat, and you have a mini-smoker. Finally, weld a firebox on one side, and a chimney on the other, and you have the design of today's modern barbecue pit. (It is interesting to note that although very little barbecue is cooked in a hole in the ground these days, the term "pit" has survived and can be used to describe any enclosed wood or charcoal-fired smoke-cooker). Put that homemade pit in the back of a pickup, head for the stadium, and you are the king of the tailgate party.

LET THE CONTESTS BEGIN!

Which brings us into the age of competitive barbecue, which in turn brings us back to Texas. In the post–Second World War oil boom, Texas was the center of the American oil industry and a huge infrastructure was built around the thousands of oil wells spurting black gold out of the ground. Oil rigs, pipelines and refineries were springing up everywhere, and many of the oil workers in Texas were also barbecue lovers. It wasn't long before some enterprising welders and pipefitters took advantage of periodic downtime in the equipment storage yard and perfected the design of the big honkin' barbecue pits you see today. These custom-built behemoths are equipped with dual wheels and towed behind the giant pickup trucks and motorhomes of barbecue fanatics and caterers who specialize in feeding Q to big crowds.

At the same time, the tradition of the tailgate party was becoming rooted in American culture. These pre-game bashes, which today often overshadow the actual football or baseball game they are celebrating, are called tailgate parties because they create a banquet table and bar out of the back of a pickup truck. In Texas, especially in the parking lot outside the Houston Astrodome, the quality of the barbecue at tailgate parties became such a source of pride that 31 years ago a bunch of Texans decided to have themselves a contest. Little did they know at the time that their little informal event would become one of the biggest barbecue contests in the world, and would spawn an entire competitive barbecue circuit, with

Photo courtesy of The Brinkman Corporation, www.thebrinkmancorp.com

governing bodies, elaborate judging criteria, and scores of championships across the continent.

Today the World's Championship Bar-B-Que is an integral part of the annual Houston Stock Show and Rodeo, with over 350 teams cooking more than 100,000 pounds (45,000 kg) of meat on giant, custom-built barbecue pits and attracting a crowd of more than 170,000 people.

BARBECUE IS HERE TO STAY

With hundreds of regional barbecue cooking contests across North America, and new barbecue restaurants springing up everywhere (there are finally a handful of authentic barbecue restaurants in New York City), barbecue has truly arrived, entering the new millennium with enough steamy smoke to power it into the future for many more generations. With strong regional styles of cooking, barbecue restaurants—both old and new—almost everywhere, and a renaissance of backyard barbecue that is giving the grill a run for its money, barbecue is here to stay. And you, dear reader, are about to become fully indoctrinated in the tools, techniques and tricks of championship barbecue.

Antioch, Illinois. In the 1950s MHP was a pioneer in decorative gas lighting for homeowners. As the market for gas lighting grew in suburban America, Walter began looking for ways to market other gas devices. After much tinkering, MHP introduced the first commercial gas grill, the Perfect Host, in 1960. The first Perfect Hosts were round and uncovered, with a cowling that held a rotisserie. The next big innovation came in 1963 when MHP introduced the first rectangular gas grill with a hinged lid—the same basic design that is now a fixture in most North American backyards. It's fun to observe that the modern covered gas grill doesn't look all that different from something one might construct out of two halves of an old oil drum!

1960—The world's first outdoor gas grill

The familiar modern gas grill

Photos courtesy of Modern Home Products, Corp.
www.modernhomeproducts.com

Championship Tools and Techniques

Chapter I

THE SCIENCE OF COOKING MEAT

s cooking techniques, grilling and barbecue are elegantly simple. You season some meat, you hold it near a fire until it's done, and then you eat it, often with your bare hands. And yet there are so many differences between how meats cook. Fish, fowl, pork, beef, lamb—all these meats have different qualities, and of course there are huge differences in taste and texture depending on what part of the animal they're from, and even from animal to animal depending on how each was raised. Barbecue champions carefully guard the sources of their meat and stay on very good terms with their butchers. (When I want a brisket for competition, my favorite butcher orders 10, calls me when they arrive and lets me pick the two I want.)

How different meats cook depends for the most part on the protein content—the fiber of the meat. Proteins consist of amino acids that are chemically bonded to form long fibers, which are in turn bundled together with connective tissue to form the muscles of an animal.

As the muscle fibers of meat are cooked, the first thing that happens is they begin to shrink and become progressively harder. Think of how soft and pliable a steak or chicken breast is when you put it on the grill, and how it quickly firms up as you cook it. This process starts at about 130°F/55°C and continues on up through to about 175°F/80°C. A perfectly done beef tenderloin has an internal temperature of about 145°F/63°C. The meat isn't raw, but it still has a lot of the tenderness that we love in rare or medium-rare beef. Now, if you were to quickly cook that tenderloin to 175°F/80°C it would seize up like a brick and the meat would turn gray. Under these conditions the proteins shrink so much that they crack and the fibers become crumbly.

So, when you grill a piece of tender, lean meat, you never want the internal temperature to go above about 160°F/71°C, and ideally you want to take it off the grill at around the 130–140°F/55–60°C range. (Except for chicken, which needs to be cooked at a slightly higher internal temperature because of risks related to salmonella.) With grilling, the goal is to get those proteins to tighten up just enough so the interior of the meat has a perfectly succulent texture—not raw, but not tough and grainy, either. The classic term is medium.

Because you don't want to overcook meat on the grill, it's a very quick cooking technique—well suited to contemporary urban life. We're so busy that the speed and convenience of grilling is hard to resist. What could be faster than seasoning a few chicken breasts and tossing them on a hot grill along with some fresh vegetables? In 10 minutes you can have a tasty meal, and there's virtually no cleanup.

THE ALCHEMY OF BARBECUE

But now, chemically speaking, it's time to bring this discussion to the next level. There's another process that begins to take place when the internal temperature of meat reaches about 150°F/66°C. It is at this point that the connective tissue—called collagen—that is holding all the protein fibers together begins to break down and turn into gelatin. This is the alchemy that makes great barbecue, and in traditional cooking it's called braising.

When meat is heated very slowly in a moist environment, the proteins don't tighten up as much, although the meat does get firm. Then, when the internal temperature slowly reaches beyond 150°F/66°C and starts approaching 170°F/77°C, something magical happens. Inside the moist interior of the meat, protected by a darkening exterior crust, the collagen starts to break down and the meat starts loosening up. The fibers relax. Juice that was squeezed out of the tissue earlier in the cooking process gets reabsorbed. Fat between the fibers liquefies and combines with the gelatin to create a rich primordial broth, basting the meat from the inside. The end result is real barbecue—the most tender, juicy, succulent meat you'll ever taste. This technique works best with meats that have a high fat content which, coincidentally, are also the cuts that have lots of connective tissue, like pork shoulders and beef briskets.

Leaner cuts simply cannot hold up to this process. Anyone who has overcooked a beef filet or top sirloin steak on an overheated grill can attest to this. With less connective tissue and a low fat content, the juices are squeezed out by overcooking and the proteins crack and crumble, leaving nothing much more than some mealy gray cardboard.

A BARBECUE EQUIPMENT PRIMER

It's difficult, but not impossible, to get a full range of cooking conditions on one piece of equipment. But to be able to use all of the grilling techniques described in this book I recommend that you have at least two cookers in your backyard: a gas or charcoal grill, and a smoker or barbecue pit. You can emulate the conditions necessary to cook real barbecue on your grill, but it's just not the same as having a smoker or pit. Have a look through this chart and you'll see what I mean. These are the four backyard cooking devices I have in my repertoire and the functions they perform.

TYPE OF COOKER	WHAT IT DOES BEST	DRAWBACKS
GAS GRILL	This is your all-purpose suburban backyard cooking device, ideal for quick grilling jobs and adaptable to bigger, more complex cooking projects like pork shoulder roasts and turkeys. Everyone should have one of these, but that doesn't mean you should use it to cook the same thing every time.	Its convenience invites laziness. With a gas grill you can have dinner in 10 minutes, and forget what you ate 10 minutes later. And natural gas and propane are odorless and tasteless. This might be an advantage if you were heating a house with them, but it's a huge liability in the flavor enhancement department. In gas-powered grills the extra flavor comes from caramelization, where your food comes into contact with the superheated grill, and the vaporized drippings, which create an interesting taste. Some extra smokey flavor can be added in the form of wood chips (see page 23).
CHARCOAL GRILL	A covered charcoal grill is superb for high-temperature grilling as well as slower indirect cooking. It has the distinct advantage of using a fuel, charcoal, that adds considerable flavor, and simply throwing some hardwood chips or chunks onto the hot briquettes can give you barbecue flavor in a shorter time than a full-blown smoker or barbecue.	The biggest drawbacks with charcoal cooking are smoke and time. Starting up a charcoal cooker can be a smokey process and if you have sensitive neighbors this can cause problems. And, of course, coals take time to start. You can't just turn on the briquettes; it takes at least 20 minutes, and more like half an hour, to start your coals and get your kettle up to temperature. For weekday family cooking this can be a non-starter unless you get into the habit of starting your coals even before you loosen your necktie!
WATER SMOKER OR HOME BARBECUE PIT	This is what you need to cook real barbecue. It produces a low heat and uses charcoal and/or hardwood to create the moist, smokey environment inside the cooking chamber that's needed to produce true Q.	Requires a fanatical devotion to barbecue. You've got to use this gear more than once a season to get good at it. The fire needs to be tended, and it takes up to 18 hours to cook some large cuts of meat. The cooker takes up space in your backyard. It generates quite a bit of smoke. It is a bit of a pain to clean up, especially after a long cooking session. It makes your wife feel like a barbecue widow. But it's worth it for the kind of fabulous food you can make!
PORTABLE GRILL	Indispensable for picnics and vacations. Allows you to bring your backyard expertise anywhere, any time.	Yet another piece of gear to irritate your spouse. Doesn't hold a huge amount of food. Hot coals can be a challenge to dispose of safely.

Always remember: take your meat off the grill before it gets to the temperature you want. It will continue to cook after you've removed it from the grill or smoker, just from the residual heat left in the meat itself. The core temperature of a prime rib roast, for example, will gain up to 15°F/9°C within a half hour of taking it out of the oven. Smaller cuts, like steaks or chicken breasts, only need to rest for 3 or 4 minutes and can be kept from cooling too quickly by loosely tenting them in foil.

Resting your meat also has another big advantage. While it's still on the grill, the juices inside are expanding with the heat, creating a good deal of pressure. By letting your meat stand for even a few minutes after taking it off the heat, you allow the pressure to subside and the interior of the meat to stabilize. The juices go back into the fibers and the meat itself firms up, sort of like a custard, resulting in a slightly denser, more silken texture when you cut it open and feel it in your mouth. Meat that has not been rested will often spurt juice when it is cut open, thereby releasing the most flavorful part of the steak all over your plate. Don't let this happen to you.

BARBECUE ❧ SECRET ❧

In competition we often wrap our brisket in foil, then in a blanket, and then place it in an insulated cooler for as many as three hours before we carve it for the judges!

If you don't want to invest in that many pieces of equipment, your best choice for versatility and flavor is a kettle-style covered charcoal grill. For convenience and speed, a gas grill can't be beat. But if you want to cook with the big boys, the minimum requirement is a bullet-style water smoker, and the ideal is a true barbecue pit, preferably one with dual wheels and your team name painted on the side!

Gas grills are designed for cooking under fairly hot temperatures. They are perfect for the kind of quick cooking that we've all grown to love. It's hard, however, to get their chamber temperature below 300°F/150°C, so they are not ideal for cooking real barbecue—although they can be put into service to produce passable pork butt and brisket.

COVERED GRILLING 101

Back in the old days of the *barbacòa*, meat was held aloft on a grate made from green wood so it wouldn't burn, with the meat sitting over the fire in the open air. The end result was probably a dry, chewy product that stored and traveled well, but wouldn't make it past the first judge in a modern barbecue competition.

Most backyard grilling today takes place on a covered grill fueled by natural gas, propane or charcoal. Almost all grills nowadays have a lid, and the manufacturers all recommend that you cook with the lid down. This creates a cooking chamber, similar to the inside of a barbecue pit, which does several things.

- **It cuts off oxygen**, which reduces flare-ups. Grease needs oxygen to burn. Anyone who has had a chicken fire on an open charcoal grill or in a drafty gas grill can attest to this.

- **It speeds up cooking time**, making your grill behave like a convection oven.

- **It allows you to cook in the rain**, or in a snowstorm, for that matter. In the Deep South, cooking on an open grill is a lot easier because the ambient temperature is so much higher and the weather is more consistently fair. It's not surprising that modern covered grilling was invented by Midwesterners!

- **It allows the food you're cooking to become infused with the aroma of the vapors inside the chamber.** This is why charcoal grilling is usually more flavorful than gas grilling. The charcoal gives off vapors that impart flavor to the food, which is further intensified by the addition of the wood chips or chunks you place on top of the coals. (This effect can be achieved to a certain extent with gas grills by putting a foil packet of water or wine-soaked wood chips directly below the grill so they produce a bit of smoke to help flavor the meat you're grilling. See more on page 23.)

The Principles of Grilling

There are basically two kinds of grilling: direct heat and indirect heat. Direct heat means cooking with the meat directly above the coals or burner. This technique allows you to cook quickly and get a nice crust on your meat. Indirect heat means cooking with the meat to the side of the coals or burner, which allows for slower cooking and avoids charring.

Within each of those broad categories, it's convenient to define three levels of heat: low, medium and high. The following chart goes into more detail.

Grilling Techniques at a Glance

DIRECT HIGH HEAT	HEAT INTENSITY	HOW IT WORKS	WHAT TO COOK
▯▯▯ *Gas or propane:* all burners on high ⬤ *Charcoal:* a full bed of hot coals	Chamber temperature 500–700°F/260–370°C for gas grills, 350–450°F/180–230°C for covered charcoal grills. (Covered gas grills can achieve much hotter chamber temperatures than charcoal grills.) *Test* You can't hold your hand directly above the grill for more than 1 or 2 seconds.	*Gas grill* The food is cooked directly above the heat source with the grill at its highest setting. *Charcoal grill* Same idea as above, but with a full, fresh hot layer of coals (about 50 briquettes, depending on the size of the cooker) under the grill and with the vents fully open.	Excellent for grilling steaks and chops and chicken parts, quickly searing tender vegetables like zucchini and asparagus, or charring slices of pineapple. Also a useful final step for crisping the skin of whatever you're cooking. Be sure to turn at least once or twice during cooking time. Only use this technique for anything that takes 10 minutes or less to cook.

NOTE

In this book it is always assumed that the cooking is taking place with the cover of the grill or smoker on. Your results will vary greatly if you grill with the lid open. The only time I would recommend grilling with the top off is for steaks or chops, on a hot, calm summer day.

The Lesson of Mom's Tough Pot ⤳ Roast ⤳

Remember the time Mom's pot roast was so tough you could hardly chew it? It's not that your Mom is a bad cook. The roast just didn't cook long enough! Pot roast is tough when it hasn't simmered long enough or has been heated too fast at the beginning of the cooking process, seizing up the meat's fibers and squeezing out all its juices. Either way, the end result is a chewy, tasteless blob of meat that belongs more on the soccer field than the plate. The same is true for undercooked barbecue, especially beef brisket and pork shoulder. These cuts should be cooked at least an hour and a half per lb./500 g over a low, smoldering fire at about 200–225°F/105°C. That means a 12-lb./5.5-kg brisket needs to cook for 18 hours! And that's why championship barbecue is an all-night affair.

DIRECT MEDIUM HEAT	HEAT INTENSITY	HOW IT WORKS	WHAT TO COOK
Gas or propane: all burners on medium	Chamber temperature 300–500°F/150–260°C.	*Gas grill* Food is cooked directly above heat source but gas adjusted to a lower setting.	This is the best all-purpose setting, suitable for almost anything. This is a gentler way to grill that just takes a little more cooking time, but it's worth it because the proteins in the meat don't seize up as much as with direct high heat. Also excellent for roasting more robust vegetables, like potatoes, squash or onions, that require a longer cooking time.
Charcoal: a medium-sized bed of hot coals	*Test* You can hold your hand directly above the grill for 3 or 4 seconds.	*Charcoal grill* Same food placement as above, with 30 or less briquettes, and the air vents adjusted as necessary.	

DIRECT LOW	HEAT INTENSITY	HOW IT WORKS	WHAT TO COOK
Gas or propane: all burners on lowest setting	Chamber temperature 200–300°F/95–150°C.	*Gas grill* Food is cooked directly above heat source but gas is adjusted to lowest possible setting.	This is good for cooking more fragile foods, like tender fish fillets, or slow-roasting bigger cuts of meat. It isn't much different from indirect medium cooking—but for a slight risk of flare-ups and a better crust.
Charcoal: a small bed of hot coals	*Test* You can hold your hand above the grill for at least 5 seconds.	*Charcoal grill* Briquettes are half spent, or use a smaller number, like 15 to 20. This style of cooking takes longer so be prepared to add a few coals every hour or so.	

INDIRECT HIGH	HEAT INTENSITY	HOW IT WORKS	WHAT TO COOK
Gas or propane: side burners on high, middle burner off with drip pan under middle grate *Charcoal:* pile of hot coals on each side of drip pan	Chamber temperature 500–700°F/260–370°C for gas grills, 350–450°F/180–230°C for covered charcoal grills.	*Gas grill* Preheat grill on high, then turn one burner off and place your meat above it. With fattier cuts you need to put a foil drip pan underneath the cooking grate to catch the drippings. *Charcoal grill* Put the coals to one side of the grill and place your meat over an aluminum pan on the other side to catch the drippings. Modern charcoal grills have special coal baskets that hold the coals on either side of the grill.	This technique is great for achieving a high cooking temperature without the risk of excessive charring or flare-ups. Great for chicken thighs and breasts, fish, steaks, racks of lamb—anything that would do well in a hot convection oven. The high heat lets you achieve a nice crust, after which you can adjust the grill to a medium heat for the rest of the cooking time.

INDIRECT MEDIUM	HEAT INTENSITY	HOW IT WORKS	WHAT TO COOK
Gas or propane: side burners on medium, middle one off *Charcoal:* medium piles of charcoal on each side of drip pan	Chamber temperature 250–350°F/120–180°C.	*Gas grill* Preheat on high, turn one burner off and place your meat above it with a drip pan if you need it. Turn down the gas on the other burner(s) to medium. *Charcoal grill* Same as indirect high, but with fewer coals and the air intake vents partially closed if necessary.	Perfect for whole chickens and turkeys, roasts—meats that require a longer cooking time.

INDIRECT LOW	HEAT INTENSITY	HOW IT WORKS	WHAT TO COOK
Gas or propane: side burners on low, middle one off *Charcoal:* small piles of charcoal on each side of drip pan	Internal temperature 180–250°F/82–120°C.	*Gas grill:* Preheat on high, turn one burner off and place your meat above it with a drip pan if you need it. Turn down the gas on the other burner(s) to as low as they will go. *Charcoal grill:* Achieve this by moderating the air intake and using a modest amount of coals.	This is where grilling and barbecue overlap, especially with the addition of some wood chips. What you have here is essentially a makeshift barbecue pit, suitable for cooking large cuts like briskets, pork shoulders and turkeys, or slow-cooking chicken, duck or other smokable foods. The big disadvantage with charcoal is you need to add more coals every hour or so.

Grilling Tips

Here are some grilling techniques that will give your backyard cooking a championship edge.

1. **Don't walk away from your grill.** I once ruined a whole grill full of kebabs because I was more interested in yakking with my friends than tending the grill. Just 2 or 3 minutes can make the difference between succulent fare and grainy, overdone meat.

2. **Don't cook everything on direct high heat.** In fact, there's almost nothing that can be cooked with direct high heat that won't improve if cooked instead for a little longer with medium heat. Super high heat is fine if you want to get nice dark char marks on your steak or zucchini, but it is a violent approach to grilling that can make the tenderest cuts of meat seize up, squeezing out their flavor-giving juices and making for mediocre food only worth eating by ravenous, boorish guests you wouldn't want back anyway. Turn the heat down. Have some patience, and get a better product! If you normally cook steaks for 4 minutes per side on a really hot grill, turn the heat to medium and try 6 minutes per side.

Instead of getting steaks that are charred to death on the outside and still cold on the inside, you'll get mouthwatering, perfectly rare or medium rare, juicy steaks that will blow your guests away.

3. **Cook on a clean, oiled, preheated grill.** I don't mean perfectly clean, like putting it through your dishwasher. Your grill should be free of gunk from the last time you cooked, and it should have some oil on it to avoid the dreaded sticking that tears the skin off chicken parts and makes fish impossible to remove. Remember these techniques for smooth, non-stick grilling.

   ◉ Always preheat your grill with a high heat for at least 5 minutes before you start cooking, then turn it down if you require a lower chamber temperature. A few minutes before you put on your food, give the grill a good scrape with a wire brush.

   ◉ Oil the grill just before cooking with a paper towel drizzled with cooking oil. Alternatively, you can spray whatever you're putting on the grill with cooking spray (like Pam or whatever else you like) on the side that will hit the grill first. Oiling the grill or the food to be grilled are sure-fire ways to prevent sticking and they don't add much extra flavor or calories to your food. (You don't have to spray the food if oil is a major ingredient in your marinade.)

4. **Turn 3 times for cool grill marks.** This is a fun technique that gets lots of oohs and aahs from your guests. Making sure you've got a hot grill, put on your steak or chop or anything else with a relatively flat surface, and turn it 3 times during cooking, rotating it 90 degrees each time you turn. You'll end up with cross-hatched grill marks like the pros.

5. **Don't turn fish at all.** Fish is such a fragile food that it can easily fall apart from excessive handling. Because a covered grill is like a convection oven, you often don't need to turn food at all for it to cook completely, especially if you use indirect heat. But this is coming from a guy with a 25-year-old grill with cooking grates that have seen better days. New grills, with nice smooth porcelain-coated cooking grates, allow you to turn fish without as much risk of sticking.

6. **Use wood chips for added flavor.** A big disadvantage of gas grills is that they don't add the classic smokey flavor to whatever you're cooking. The more expensive gas grills often have a special little chamber for wood chips, which emulate the smokey environment inside a barbecue pit, but you can adapt any covered gas grill in this way:

   Step 1 Presoak a handful of hardwood chips (see chart, pages 25–26, for the kinds of flavors they impart) in water, wine or apple juice and then wrap them in foil to make a kind of packet.

   Step 2 Poke some holes in the packet with a fork and toss the bag onto the lava rocks or spatter guards underneath your cooking grate. They will soon begin to smolder and give off smoke.

   Step 3 When the packet is throwing off a good amount of smoke, put your food on the grill and it will take on a bit of smokey flavor. It ain't real barbecue, but it's better than nothin'—and if you get good at it, you can actually create a modest smoke ring using a gas grill!

BARBECUE ⮞ SECRETS ⮜

Let the food cook a bit before you try to turn it. An uncooked burger patty has a much higher chance of sticking to the grill than one that has started to firm up.

⮞ ⮜

Flip your meat onto an unused part of the grill for maximum searing power and the best grill marks. The metal that your meat is touching will be cooled by the liquid in the meat. A dry, hot grill makes the darkest char marks! Also, if you want nice dark grill marks, use a rub that has at least a little sugar in it.

⮞ ⮜

Always cook fish skin-side down. When it's done, you can use a spatula to lift the fish right off its skin, which will stick to the grill. As a bonus snack, grill the skin for a few minutes, then pry it off with a spatula and sprinkle with salt. It's crispy and chewy good—the bacon of the sea!

Duelling
⮞ Definitions ⮜

Webster's New World Dictionary, Second College Edition

barbecue / (bär be kyoo)) n. [Sp. *Barbacoa* < framework of sticks] 1. orig., a raised framework for smoking, drying or broiling meat 2. a hog, steer, etc. broiled or roasted whole over an open fire, sometimes in an open pit 3. any meat broiled on a spit over an open fire 4. a party or picnic at which such meat is served 5. a restaurant that specializes in barbecuing 6. a portable outdoor grill—vt. -cued, -cuing 1. to prepare (meat) outdoors by roasting on a spit or broiling on a grill, usually over a charcoal fire 2. to broil or cook (meat) with a highly seasoned sauce (barbecue sauce) containing vinegar, tomatoes, spices, etc.

Rockin' Ronnie's New Dictionary of Barbecue

barbecue / (bawr buh kyoo) n. [Amer. *Barbecue* < greatest food on earth] 1. a big, fat, tough piece of meat cooked for a long time over low heat using a charcoal or hardwood fire until it is tender and succulent 2. the inspiration for a subculture of barbecue enthusiasts who go from city to city all summer, competing for who can cook the ultimate piece of meat 3. the basis of a restaurant with Formica tables, bad lighting and watery draft beer that serves big portions of barbecue to happy but overweight patrons 4. a way of life, emphasizing the consumption of barbecue, drinking, storytelling and card playing.

CLASSIC BARBECUE 101

Okay. This is it. Now that you have mastered the backyard art of grilling, it's time to graduate to the big time. This is barbecue, the noun ("Rockin' Ronnie cooks great barbecue"), as opposed to barbecue, the verb ("Honey let's barbecue some pork chops"), is the kind of barbecue people in the American South travel hours to eat. It is the source of fierce rivalries and friendly arguments. It can convert vegetarians, make women swoon and men grunt with delight. And, yes, you can cook it in your own backyard. But pay attention. While this isn't rocket science, it's a lot different from searing a rib steak on your gas grill.

Principles of Barbecue

Barbecue is one of the simplest and oldest ways of preparing meat. All you need for cooking are three basic components: low heat, hardwood smoke and time. Almost anything can be prepared in this way, from classic chicken, pork and beef dishes to fresh tomatoes, onions and hard-boiled eggs.

You can get as fancy as you want when it comes to spicing and saucing your meat. Many traditionalists don't use barbecue sauce at all, or might use it sparingly at the end of cooking as a finishing glaze. Barbecue sauce is often referred to as "dipping sauce" as a way of purposely relegating it to a minor role, as an optional accompaniment to barbecued meat.

The classic way to turn meat into barbecue is to coat it with prepared mustard and then sprinkle on a dry rub made from salt, sugar and spices. You can add your personal signature to barbecued meat through the kind of hardwood you choose and the spice combination in the rub. That said, for many pit masters, particularly in Texas, land of the brisket, the only way to cook barbecue is to put the meat in the pit with nothing on it and just cook it for a long time. The smoke provides so much flavor and the texture is so succulent that salt and sugar and spices seem redundant!

Flavoring with Wood: A Rough-Hewn Guide

Unless you have a giant barbecue pit that is fuelled by hardwood logs, the basic technique for creating classic barbecue flavor is to place two or three chunks of wood on top of your hot coals. The heat from the coals makes the wood smolder and burn, creating the precious vapor that flavors your food. Always use dry, untreated woods for cooking. Green wood generates creosote when it is burned, which is not good.

Hardwood chunks last longer than chips, but their smoke is less intense. Soak hardwood in water or wine before using if you want to generate more smoke, but be careful. You can oversmoke things, imparting a bitter, acrid aftertaste to your food. Try to use wood chunks that don't have a lot of thick bark, which can make for bitter smoke. If you're burning logs in a pit, burn off the bark before you put your meat in the smoker.

WOOD	FLAVOR / AROMA	USES
HICKORY	The classic sweet, strong smell and hearty taste of American barbecue, this is the wood used in the original American pig roasts of the sixteenth century. Hickory smoke is so pervasive a flavor in North America today that sometimes we forget where it comes from. Whenever you see "smoke" on the ingredient list in wieners, bacon or ham, it's probably hickory.	You can't go wrong with hickory. It goes well with everything from pork to chicken and salmon. The only problem: some say it makes everything taste like ham! It is truly one of the "comfort food" flavors.
MESQUITE	A strong, heavy, pungent, slightly acrid aroma that imparts a classic Southwestern flavor to smoked and wood-grilled foods. Burns hot, so watch how much you use.	Use it for smoking beef, game, duck, lamb, or any of the more strongly flavored meats. Great grilling wood for almost anything. Your favorite Tex-Mex restaurant probably cooks your steak with it.
OAK	Lovely dry, nutty aroma, with a slight but noticeable acidity. Available plain, as well as in the chopped-up remains of wine and liquor barrels, which add another layer of flavor and complexity.	Excellent for beef brisket, but great with almost anything except maybe fish. Perhaps the most versatile hardwood.
MAPLE	Mild, sweet, reminiscent of the smell of a fireplace at a fishing lodge.	Goes well with poultry, ham and vegetables. Some brands of bacon are maple-smoked.
ALDER	Fresh, pungent, dry aroma, mild flavor.	The classic way to smoke salmon.
PECAN	Similar to hickory but milder and cooler burning. Popular among competitors as well as professional chefs.	Use instead of hickory, maple or oak as an all-purpose cooking wood.
BIRCH AND WILLOW	Sharply aromatic, pungent, the closest thing to softwood in a hardwood. Scorned by some but used by others, particularly above the Mason-Dixon line.	Fish and game.
APPLE, CHERRY, PEACH	Sweet, mild, fruity, very smooth.	Great with pork and poultry but they go with almost anything. Also good to blend with other woods, like hickory or oak.
GRAPEVINE	Rich, fruity, aromatic.	Game, lamb or fish.
CEDAR	A softwood that imparts a distinctive, sharp, astringent aroma and flavor to meat.	Requires a special technique: planking (see page 175). Excellent with fish but also great with cheese, fruits and vegetables.

The North Carolina Pork Producers

barbecue / 1. the premier ethnic food of North Carolina 2. pig pickin' 3. catalyst for great debate 4. a method of cooking 5. pig as a culinary art 6. a cultural rite 7. all of the above.

Kansas City Barbecue Society

"Barbecue is meat cooked by indirect heat and smoke."

Kenny Callaghan, pitmaster of Blue Smoke, New York City's premier barbecue restaurant as quoted in the *New York Times*

"How about this. Once you've been to your fiftieth or sixtieth barbecue joint, you just know what barbecue is."

Chris Schlesinger, from the foreword of *Smoke and Spice*

"…next to survival, fellowship is the main purpose of cooking and eating. People spending time together while preparing food and eating—this is the essence of barbecue…."

Journalist Jonathan Daniels, writing in the mid-twentieth century

"Barbecue is the dish which binds together the taste of both the people of the big house and the poorest occupants of the back end of the broken-down barn."

Hardwood's ⇒ Magical Vapors ⇐

There is nothing like the aroma and taste of real barbecue. You can smell a good barbecue restaurant from a mile away. That smell is hardwood smoke, which does some magical things in the chamber of a barbecue pit. At the same time as the fat in the meat is liquefying and the connective tissue is breaking down, the hardwood that is slowly burning to produce the heat is also throwing off beautiful vapors called aromatic hydrocarbons. A hardwood fire is nothing more than the combination of oxygen with the organic compounds of the wood, the main by-products being carbon dioxide and water vapor. But, because of the low heat, the wood is not fully combusted, resulting in the microscopic particles we call smoke, along with the invisible, but crucial, aromatics. Interestingly, a smoker that is working properly does not produce very much actual smoke. Rather, the temperature is high enough that the wood burns with a very controlled flame, rather than smoldering, which produces more smoke than vapor.

Meats cooked with too smokey a fire blacken quickly and have a bitter, acrid crust. Meats cooked in an ideal, vapor-filled environment develop a mahogany brown exterior crust over time, and the interior of the meat becomes infused with the hardwood fumes, taking on the essential aroma and flavor of the wood itself. Burn fruitwood like cherry, apple or peach in your smoker and the meat takes on a wonderful smokey sweetness. Use hickory for the classic taste of barbecue that goes back to the

WOOD	FLAVOR / AROMA	USES
DRIED CORNCOBS	Sweet, mild.	Use them like you would a fruitwood for poultry or pork, or combine with a heartier wood like maple or oak.
SEAWEED	Tangy, salty, smokey (or so it's said).	Shellfish and all kinds of seafood. Wash and dry before use.
HERBS (bay leaves, cinnamon sticks, whole nutmeg) and herb wood (branches of rosemary, sage, thyme)	A whole other level of flavor more often used in Europe than in America. Try it some time! Rosemary adds a piney aroma to lamb.	Lamb and fish, vegetables, cheeses.

Barbecue Techniques for Backyard Cooks

The first thing you need is a water smoker (unless you can shell out a lot of money for a traditional-style barbecue pit, with a side-mounted firebox and a built-in well for water). Water smokers come in many different styles, but most are basically alike, designed in a classic egg shape, resembling Star Wars' famous droid, R2D2. They cost anywhere from $50 to $300. All of them will do the job. Weber and Brinkman make good ones, the Weber Smokey Mountain Cooker being the standard equipment for competitive barbecuers who can't afford big custom pits.

You don't need many tools in addition to your water smoker. Truth be told, you can make do with a good long pair of tongs, some old oven mitts and a charcoal chimney for starting your coals. But who wants to go with the minimum requirement? (See pages 33–35 for a gearhead's guide.)

Getting Started

At the bottom of the water smoker is a basket for your charcoal and hardwood chunks. Better models have adjustable vents to help control air flow and temperature. It's best to get your coals going in a chimney-style starter before you put them in the smoker. Charcoal chimneys are designed so you put charcoal briquettes in the chimney and place one or two crumpled pieces of newspaper in a chamber at the bottom. You light the newspaper, and about 15 minutes later you have nice hot briquettes. Never use lighting fluid or any other chemical starter. It can alter the taste of the meat.

How much charcoal you use depends on how long you're going to be cooking, and one full chimney of briquettes is not really enough to cook anything other than maybe some chicken pieces or a couple of racks of lamb. The trick is to put a layer of cold briquettes in the basket and then pour your hot ones on top to begin. When I'm barbecuing a brisket or pork butt I start out with 10 to 15 lbs./ 4.5 to 6.75 kg of coals.

The Water Pan
In your smoker, just above where the coals go, there's a water pan. The water helps keep the meat moist and also maintains the internal temperature of the smoker at an ideal 200–225°F/95–105°C. When you fill up this bowl-shaped receptacle, it's best if you first coat it with a double layer of extra-wide foil for ease of cleanup later. Use hot tap water to fill the water pan. (We like to use apple juice in competition.) If you want to get fancy, throw in a bottle or two of dark beer, some wine, or whatever you've been marinating your meat in. Some very fatty cuts of meat, such as pork shoulder butt, can be cooked at a slightly higher temperature (250°F/120°C) with a drier heat. In cases like this you can leave the water pan in the smoker without any water in it to catch the drippings.

Be sure you monitor your water level. For long smoking jobs you may need to add water to the pan once or twice.

Preparing the Meat: Mustard and Rub
Take the meat you are going to smoke out of the fridge and let it sit for an hour or so at room temperature. Coat the meat on both sides with a thin layer of prepared mustard (not fancy Dijon, just plain old ballpark mustard). Sprinkle dry rub (see Dry Rub Recipes, pages 50–55) on the meat, giving it a nice even distribution. (If the meat has been brined or heavily marinated, you can often do without the mustard and rub.)

Let the rubbed meat sit for 15 minutes or until tacky (the salt in the rub starts to draw the moisture out of the meat). Place the meat fat side up on the grill of your smoker, put some hardwood on the coals and let it cook at 200–225°F/95–105°C.

Monitoring the Temperature inside the Cooking Chamber
Above the charcoal and the water pan are two circular cooking grates on which you place your meat once you've got your smoker up to temperature. Some cheap water smokers come with a temperature gauge, usually one that says WARM, IDEAL AND HOT. This is not good enough. Buy a good metal probe-style thermometer that goes from 100–500°F/38–260°C. If you don't have an air vent at the top of your smoker, make one with a drill. When the temperature reaches 200–225°F/95–105°C it's time to put your meat in.

Tending Your Meat
Once you have put your meat on the grill, put some hardwood chips or chunks on the coals (see page 24) and put the cover on your smoker. Some barbecue cooks like to soak their wood chunks or wood chips in water or wine for at least a couple of hours before using them. The wet wood produces more smoke; for a milder

plentiful hickory forests of the east coast. Or burn mesquite for the dark, sharp, tangy flavor of traditional Texas barbecue.

Barbecue competitors often have their own custom mix of hardwoods to add to the richness and complexity of the meat they're cooking. I like to use a combination of cherry, hickory and mesquite for the bigger cuts like pork butt and brisket, and pure fruitwoods for ribs and chicken to enhance their natural sweetness and not overpower the meat flavor.

Most big barbecue pits run on pure wood—hickory, pecan or oak logs are favorites. But home cooks who use smaller cookers usually start with a base of charcoal briquettes and then toss hardwood chunks or chips on top of the briquettes to create the vapors essential to classic barbecue.

Where can you find hardwood to fuel your backyard barbecue passion? Sometimes you can find it in someone's backyard. My cherry wood comes from a friend who chopped down a cherry tree as part of a home landscaping project. But most barbecue supply stores and general hardware/building supply outlets have bags of hardwood chunks and chips in the same place they sell grills and grilling utensils. If you want to source hardwood logs or more obscure woods, call around to some high-end restaurants in your city; local chefs who use wood-fired ovens often know where to get the best cooking woods.

flavor, don't soak. Now it's time for a long break. The key to great barbecue is to let the cooker do the work. The more you open the smoker to check, the longer the cooking time. Every time you open your smoker, you add about 15 minutes to your cooking time.

Allow 1½ or 2½ hours for hamburgers, 2½ to 3 hours for half chickens, 5 or 6 hours for ribs, 1½ hours per lb./500 g for pork shoulder or beef brisket. Add more hardwood to the coals every hour or two.

MASTER BARBECUE CHART

This chart is designed as a guide for cooking barbecue in a water smoker or a barbecue pit, assuming the internal temperature of the cooker is about 200–220°F/95–100°C.

You can emulate this technique in a gas grill by using indirect low heat, placing a drip pan underneath fattier cuts of meat, and wrapping soaked wood chips in foil and placing them directly over a burner. In all cases make sure to let the meat rest, tented in foil, for at least 15 minutes for small cuts and an hour or more for bigger ones.

MEAT	SIZE	BEST HARD-WOOD FLAVORS	COOKING TIME AND DONENESS TEST
PORK			
Pork butt (bone in)	6–8 lbs./2.7–3.5 kg	Hickory, oak, apple, cherry	1½ hours per lb./3 hours per kg. Butt is done when the internal temperature reaches 185°F/85°C.
Pork loin (boneless)	3–5 lbs./1.4–2.2 kg	See above	3 to 5 hours or until the internal temperature reaches 145°F/63°C.
Ribs (side ribs or baby backs)	Full slab	See above	4 to 6 hours or to an internal temperature of 165°F/74°C. Ribs should pull easily away from the bone.
Pork sausage raw (like bratwurst, chorizo or Italian)	1-inch/2.5-cm. diameter	See above	2 to 3 hours until sausages are firm and no longer pink in the center (about 150–160°F/66–71°C).
BEEF			
Boneless roasts (sirloin, tri-tip, rib, cross-rib)	4–6 lbs./1.8–2.7 kg	Hickory, mesquite, oak, cherry	About 1 hour to the lb./2 hours per kg or until internal temperature reads 125°F/52°C for rare, 140°F/60°F for medium rare. Not worth eating if they're well done!

MEAT	SIZE	BEST HARD-WOOD FLAVORS	COOKING TIME AND DONENESS TEST
BEEF (cont'd)			
Brisket	10–14 lb./4.5–6.5 kg	Hickory, mesquite, oak, cherry	Cook 1½ hours per lb./3 hours per kg, until internal temperature reads 85°F/85°C. When you lift the roast to turn it, it should have a relaxed, jelly-like feeling. It is underdone if it feels very firm and tight.
Short ribs	2–3 inches/5–8 cm thick	See above	3 to 4 hours or until meat pulls easily off the bone.
Prime rib bones	Rack with 6–8 bones	See above	3 to 4 hours or until internal temperature at the thickest part of the ribs reaches 140°F/60°C for medium rare.
Hamburgers	⅓–½ lb./150–250 g each	See above	Yes, you can smoke hamburgers. Cook for 1½ to 2½ hours until the internal temperature reaches 150°F/66°C for medium rare, or until the burgers become springy but not hard when touched. If you like, you can coat them with barbecue sauce and finish them on a hot grill.
POULTRY			
Turkey, whole (no stuffing, cavity open to allow smoke to circulate)	10–12 lbs./4.5–5.5 kg	Apple, cherry, grapevine, oak, hickory	7 or 8 hours or until internal temperature at the thigh joint is 160°F/71°C.
Chicken, halves, cut in half lengthwise	3–5 lbs./1.4–2.2 kg	See above	2½ to 3 hours or until internal temperature at the thigh joint is 160°F/71°C or until meat near the thighbone is no longer pink (cut to test).
Duck, whole, cut in half lengthwise	4–6 lbs./2–2.7 kg	Apple, cherry	4 to 6 hours until temperature at the thickest part of the breast is 160°F/71°C.
Cornish game hen	1–1½ lbs./500–750 g	See above	2 to 3 hours or until the meat next to the thigh bone is no longer pink (cut to test).
LAMB			
Leg, bone in	4–6 lbs./1.8–2.7 kg	Apple, cherry, oak	1 hour per lb./2 hours per kg, or until the internal temperature reaches 140°F/60°C for medium rare.
Shoulder, whole, bone in	3–4 lbs./1.5–2 kg	See above	5 to 7 hours or until internal temperature reaches 170°F/77°C and meat pulls easily off the bone.
Rack, whole	1.5–2 lbs./750 g–1 kg	See above, but also try a few rosemary branches	1½ to 2 hours or until the internal temperature reaches 125°F/52°C for rare, 140°F/60°F for medium rare. Not worth eating well done!
FISH			
Whole, small	1 lb./500 g	Alder, grapevine, hickory, oak	¾ to 1½ hours or until flesh is just starting to firm up and almost flakes.

The Smoke ⤜ Ring ⤚

Judges in barbecue competitions look for something called a "smoke ring" when meat is presented to them. This bright pink ring is the evidence of the depth of penetration of the aromatics into the meat. The more pronounced the smoke ring, the better. The reddish color is caused by nitrogen compounds in the smoke reacting with myoglobin, the oxygen carrying protein in muscle tissue. Nitrates not only color the meat but also act as a natural preservative, inhibiting bacterial growth. Ever wonder why ham is pink? It's because nitrates are added to commercial meat products. Rumor has it that some modern barbecue competitors add powdered nitrates to their rubs to artificially enhance their smoke rings—a travesty, as far as most competitors are concerned! Many barbecue restaurants publish warnings to guests who are new to barbecue and might mistake the red color of their ribs or beef for raw or undercooked meat. With barbecue, if it's got a red ring, it's done like dinner!

Emulating Real Barbecue on Your Covered Gas Grill

Real barbecue takes three essential components: time, low heat and smoke. This makes it difficult, but not impossible, to approximate real barbecue on a gas grill. Here's how to do it.

1. Use indirect low heat. Put a foil pan underneath the cooking grate on one side of your grill to catch the drippings. Preheat the grill by turning on the burner on

MEAT	SIZE	BEST HARD-WOOD FLAVORS	COOKING TIME AND DONENESS TEST
FISH (cont'd)			
Whole fillet (side), large	3–4 lbs./1.5–1.8 kg	Alder, grapevine, hickory, oak. If you're cooking salmon, use hickory or alder for best results	2 to 3 hours or until flesh is just starting to firm up and almost flakes.
Fillets or steaks	6–8 oz./170–227 g per piece	Alder, grapevine, hickory, oak.	1 to 1½ hours or until flesh is just starting to firm up and almost flakes.
Shellfish—oysters, scallops, prawns	1–2 oz./25–50 g per piece	Alder, grapevine, hickory, oak	½ to 1 hour, until they are just heated through and firm to the touch.
VEGETABLES			
Tomatoes	Medium-sized	Hickory, oak, apple, cherry	½ hour or until the tomatoes start to take on a golden tinge but are still firm to the touch.
Onion	Peeled and cut into ¼–½-inch/5–10-mm rounds	See above	About an hour or until it takes on a golden color.
Red bell pepper	Medium size, nice and meaty	See above	¾ to 1½ hours or until flesh is soft.
Garlic	Whole head, trimmed to expose the cloves	Apple or cherry	2 to 3 hours or until head is golden brown and garlic is soft and tender.
MISCELLANEOUS			
Salt (kosher, Malden or fleur de sel sea salt)	1 cup / 250 mL spread evenly in a cake pan or pie plate	Hickory, oak, apple or cherry	About 1 hour, stirring once or twice, until salt is golden brown.
Nuts whole shelled pecans, almonds or your favorite nut	½ lb./250 g spread evenly in a cake pan or pie plate	See above	1 hour or until the nuts have taken on a slightly darker hue.
Cheese (mozzarella, Jack, Gouda, Cheddar, or any other firm cheese)	½ lb./250 g wrapped in cheesecloth	See above	1 to 2 hours.

A BACKYARD COOK'S PANTRY

This is not a comprehensive list of everything you need in your grilling and barbecue arsenal. But these are a few of my favorite ingredients—some more obscure than others—all of which I consider essential to great backyard cooking.

Asian sauces: Light and dark soy, toasted sesame oil, oyster sauce, black bean sauce and chili garlic sauce should be in your pantry. Use them in marinades, combine them to make an Asian finishing glaze, doctor mayo for a flavorful dip, or just paint them on meat as you grill it.

Black peppercorns: If you haven't already done so, please throw out any prepackaged ground pepper in your pantry. Pepper loses its aromatic oils shortly after being ground, so always use whole peppercorns and grind them in a pepper mill. If you need a large amount, use a spice mill or coffee grinder. Use finely ground pepper in rubs and a coarser grind for coating steaks and roasts.

Chiles, ground: Dried chiles are some of the essential flavor components of great barbecue. Use them in everything: sauces, marinades, rubs, dips and dressings. Cut half and half with kosher salt and sprinkle on hot buttered corn on the cob. Add to guacamole and salsa for extra flavor and heat. Be sure to use the real stuff—don't waste your money on store-bought blended chili powder.

Chipotles in adobo sauce: This is common in Latin American pantries and widely available in the Mexican food section of most supermarkets. Dried chipotles are reconstituted and stewed in a tomato-based sauce and packaged in little tins. One or two chipotles adds a wonderful hot, smokey flavor to sauces and marinades.

Cooking spray: For spraying grills and food about to go on the grill.

Cumin seeds: Raw cumin seeds are available just about everywhere these days, and you can buy big bags of them in the Indian spices section of your supermarket. This is one of my favorite spices, with a dark, earthy, slightly smokey taste and pungent aroma. Use them whole to add an interesting texture to dishes and give a little burst of flavor when you bite into them. For most uses I recommend toasting cumin seeds just before adding them to whatever you're cooking (see toasting, page 68). There's nothing like freshly toasted cumin seeds ground in a spice mill or coffee grinder!

Extra virgin olive oil: There isn't much room for olive oil in traditional barbecue, but for grilled foods there's nothing like a last-minute drizzle of fruity extra virgin olive oil and a squeeze of lemon to brighten the flavors and enhance the richness of your cooking.

Flavored oils: French toasted walnut oil, truffle oil, lime-infused olive oil and chili-flavored oil add so much to salads and marinades, making it easy to add a distinctive and unusual flavor to everyday fare.

the other side on high for 5 minutes, then turning it to its lowest setting. Ideally you want the chamber temperature to be somewhere in the range of 200–250°F/95–120°C. Place whatever you're cooking (like a pork butt or brisket) on the grate on the cool side of the grill, above the drip pan. Then cook as if it were in a smoker or barbecue pit, turning periodically and spraying with apple juice.

2. Generate some smoke to help flavor the meat. Take some hardwood chips or chunks and soak them in water for about an hour. Wrap them in a double coating of foil to make a neat packet. Pierce the packet with a fork in a few places and then place the packet on the hot side of your grill over top your lava rocks or drip guard. The wood will heat up and slowly burn, releasing smoke into the chamber of your grill, giving the meat a bit of smokey flavor and producing a mild red smoke ring.

3. Use smoked salt in your rub or paint your meat with a little liquid smoke before you cook it. You can also put some smoke flavor in your finishing glaze. This technique is heresy to barbecue aficionados but it's better than nothing.

If you want real barbecue flavor, especially for bigger cuts of meat, spend a few hundred dollars on the right cooking machine and I promise that you and your guests won't regret it!

A ground chile ⊱ primer ⊰

Store-bought chili powder tastes okay if you don't know what tastes better. But once you have used real ground chiles in your cooking, you'll never go back to the store-bought stuff, which does contain ground dried chiles but usually also contains table salt and other spices, like oregano and cumin. It's well worth the trouble to find a Latin specialty grocer that carries a selection of real powdered chiles. I like to use a combination of different powdered chiles in my rubs. Here are my favorites.

Ancho, the mildest, sweetest of the dried chiles, has a rich, dark, red-brown color, and a mild, fruity flavor with overtones of coffee, raisin and tobacco.

Cayenne, the ubiquitous source of heat in so many styles of cooking, has a pungent, tart heat that adds a little undercurrent of excitement to almost any food.

Chipotle, a very flavorful chile made from dried smoked jalapeños, has tobacco and chocolate overtones and a strong, even heat.

New Mexico Chipotle has a classic mild, earthy flavor and a nice crisp heat.

Guajillo is a sharp, tannic chile with lots of heat.

Pasilla has a dark, herbal flavor.

Paprika is made from sweet red chiles and has a lovely mild flavor and beautiful red color.

Smoked paprika, the European cousin to chipotle powder, is one of the signature flavors in the classic Spanish rice dish paella, but also makes a great component of a barbecue rub.

A couple of spoonfuls of flavored oil, a squeeze of fresh lemon or lime juice, a little dollop of Dijon, some finely minced shallot and a pinch of salt and pepper makes a quick dressing that will amaze your guests.

Granulated garlic and onion: Lots of cooks frown on powdered seasonings and I don't blame them. They can often taste rancid and bitter, especially when they're not fresh. But granulated garlic and onion are different. They have a wonderful texture and a rich, roasted taste that adds an intense flavor to grilled and barbecued food. I find myself adding a bit of granulated onion to almost everything I cook nowadays for an extra dimension of flavor.

Herbs, dried: The modern kitchen tends to shy away from dried herbs in favor of their aromatic and delicate fresh counterparts, but good dried herbs (that is, ones that haven't spent the last seven years in the back of your spice cupboard) add a richness and complexity to food that fresh herbs can't. I often like to combine fresh herbs with their dried counterparts to create a big, balanced flavor with an earthy, bitter bottom and a crisp aromatic brightness.

Ketchup: This gives Kansas City–style sauces their classic sweetness and glossy, thick texture.

Kosher salt: Please, please, please throw out all your cheap iodized salt, which is too powdery and has a chemical aftertaste from the iodine that is added to prevent goiter. Trust me. You're not going to get goiter. I'm sure we all get enough iodine from the salt in the processed food we eat! You can get kosher salt at almost any specialty food shop, and in many supermarkets these days. Be sure you get a brand like Diamond Crystal—some kosher salts are very coarse and are used mainly for pickling. The kind of Kosher salt I'm talking about has a slightly coarser, more granular quality than regular table salt, which gives it a subtle crunchy texture when sprinkled on food just before you serve it. Kosher salt also has a less salty, more well-rounded flavor. If you want to get even fancier, use lovely white crystalline Malden salt from England, or grayish-brown, minerally fleur de sel from France, for putting that finishing sprinkle on food just before you serve it.

Lemons and limes: Don't bother with bottled lime or lemon juice. The real thing is so much better! Always keep a few of each of these on hand to add tang to a sauce or salad, to squeeze over meat or vegetables fresh off the grill, or to chew on between shots of tequila!

Mustard: Good old ballpark-style prepared mustard is an essential component of barbecued meat, but you should also have some Dijon in your fridge. Flavored mustards like wasabi lime or honey mustard add a nice twist to marinades, mayo and dressings. Grainy mustard gives sauces and glazes an extra bit of texture.

Nuts: I like to keep bags of pecan halves, pine nuts, pumpkin seeds and slivered almonds in the freezer. Quickly toast them in a frying pan or put them on a cookie sheet for a few minutes under your broiler and sprinkle them on a salad or piece of grilled fish to add some crunch and flavor.

Seasoned salts: Garlic salt, onion salt, celery salt and steak-house seasoning salt are important components of barbecue rubs.

Sours: White vinegar, cider vinegar, red and white wine vinegars and balsamic vinegar are good to have around. It's all about the balance of salt, sour, bitter, sweet and savory. Great barbecue would not be complete without an acidic tang.

Sweets: Honey, maple syrup, white sugar, brown sugar and molasses add an important dimension to sauces, marinades and dressings.

YOU NEED GEAR ...
LOTS AND LOTS OF BARBECUE GEAR!

I. Backyard essentials. If you're serious about backyard cooking, here is the must-have gear list.

Basting brushes: Natural bristle paint brushes work better than the basting brushes normally available in grocery stores. You need a range of sizes.

Carving knife: Get a long-bladed chef's knife with a good grip. Many competitors use a super-long ham knife to carve their meat for judging.

Charcoal chimney: This is an essential component of any charcoal-based system. (Don't get the kind that automatically releases your charcoal when you lift it up!)

Cutting boards: You need two at home—a big one for carving and a smaller one, with a handle, for those little chopping jobs. In competition it's good to have four or five in a variety of sizes.

Filleting knife: The short, flexible blade makes it easy to remove chicken breasts from the bone and trim fat off briskets and pork butts.

Fire starter: Although some of my teammates have no problem with stinky liquid fire starter, I prefer the chemical-free ones like wax-impregnated felt sticks. I use these instead of newspaper at the bottom of my charcoal chimney because they generate less smoke.

Grill scraper: Essential for quickly and easily getting the crud off the grill from your last cooking session. I prefer the metal brushes but the scouring pad–style ones also work fine.

Matches: Nothing worse than running out of matches. Keep a box of wooden matches handy and hide a backup somewhere else.

⤙ **Barbecue-mami!** ⤚

There is a lot of talk these days of a fifth taste (different from sour, salt, bitter and sweet) that is related to glutamate, an amino acid found in meat, fish and legumes. Some call it savory, and the Japanese have named it umami. An artificial version of this taste, in the form of monosodium glutamate, is used in many manufactured foods and almost every salty snack you can buy. According to experts, glutamates increase salivation and enhance the salty and sweet flavors of foods. Soy sauce, reduced chicken stock, peas and seaweed are all rich in umami flavor.

And then, of course, there's the heat in chiles, called capsaicin, an odorless, tasteless chemical that stimulates our taste buds and intensifies all the other tastes.

I like to think of barbecue as the ultimate combination of all the five tastes, enhanced by chile heat, with the most glorious texture of perfectly cooked meat. Call it barbecue-mami.

At least two pairs: one ratty old pair for handling greasy grills and lifting and turning extra-large cuts, and a nicer pair for pulling side dishes and appetizers out of the oven.

Poultry shears: Good to have around for cutting up chickens and ducks.

Resealable plastic bags: Use them for marinating, storing, transporting. Always get the extra-thick freezer bags. Have medium, large and extra large on hand at all times.

Rib racks: These wire frames are extremely handy if you want to cook more than three or four racks of ribs.

Spatula: This is a must for flipping burgers and lifting anything fragile, like fish fillets, off the grill. The bigger the better, and you should probably have at least two so you can get bigger pieces of fish off the grill in one piece.

Spice mill: Freshly ground spices, especially black pepper and cumin, are so much better than the ones you buy in a jar. A coffee grinder is the perfect device for this.

Thermometers: You need two kinds.

- A barbecue thermometer gauges the chamber temperature inside your covered grill, water smoker or barbecue pit. These usually go from 140–600°F/60–315°C. This is an essential tool and can range from a simple backyard model to industrial-style gauges used by pitmasters and barbecue competitors. The bigger and more expensive your thermometer, the more reliable—and the better to intimidate your opponents.

- An instant-read meat thermometer, preferably a digital one, is an extremely important tool for judging the doneness of your meat. Digital ones are more reliable than the fairly fragile analog versions.

Tongs: You need a good pair—the kind with soft rubber grips and a smooth spring action—for cooking, and a crappy pair (any kind will do as long as they are long) for handling coals and moving around grills.

II: For barbecue gearheads and die-hard contest entrants, this is the enhanced list.

Alka-Seltzer: Say no more.

Bear paws: A specialized tool for shredding pork, available from barbecue specialty stores and online through sites like bulkbbq.com, barbecue-store.com and hawgeyesbbq.com/.

Brine pump or syringe: Many barbecue champions, particularly in the pork category, inject a mixture of fruit juice, salt and seasonings into the meat to enhance its succulence. You can do this on smaller roasts with a cooking syringe, or if you want to literally go whole hog

Grilling and Barbecuing ➤ Indoors ≈

So you live in an apartment that doesn't allow gas or charcoal griling on your balcony. Or you don't have a balcony. Or you live on another planet. Well, you can still grill and barbecue in your kitchen. For about $100 you can buy an electric grill or you can use a stovetop grilling pan. And you can even add a smokey flavour to a smaller piece of meat by putting some hardwood chips in the bottom of a wok and putting the meat on a metal steaming grate. Close the wok, heat it up til smoke comes out and voila. (Be sure you do this in a well-ventilated kitchen with a fan above the stove and a fire extinguisher nearby.)

you need a brine pump, which looks like a horse needle attached to a bicycle pump. My team doesn't do this, but if you're game, get a syringe and experiment!

Card table: See cribbage board.

Coolers: Everyone's got one of these at home, but for competition you need at least four: one for storing raw meat, one for keeping wine and beer, one for lettuce, parsley, butter and other groceries, and one for keeping your briskets and pork butts warm while they rest before being carved and turned in to the judges.

Cribbage board: This, especially when accompanied by Jack Daniel's and Coke, is the competitive barbecuer's best friend. Excellent for passing the hours between spraying your meat and checking your coals.

Duct tape, shock cord, pliers, scissors, wire, bungee cords: You never know.

Extra batteries: Have these on hand in case your digital thermometer runs out of steam just before turn-in-time, or your flashlight goes dead.

Flashlight: A late-night tool for checking coals, adding water to the water pan and finding the corkscrew.

Gazebo-style tent: Protects you from the sun and the rain. It rains at barbecue competitions almost as often as the peanut butter side of your bread hits the ground first.

Heat-resistant silicone oven mitts: If you've got the dough, these high-tech mitts withstand up to 600 degrees of heat. They look cool, too.

Knife-sharpening gear: Next to Alka-Seltzer, a sharp knife is a cook's best friend. I carry a knife-sharpening system with five different grains of oilstones. You should also have a steel honing device for putting a razor edge on your knives just before using them.

Old blanket: For wrapping pork butts and briskets that have long resting times.

Portable lawn chairs: Excellent for playing cards and napping.

Portable paper towel dispenser: Along with vinyl gloves, a critical tool to enhance speed and hygiene.

Remote digital meat probe: Barbecue competitors are always trying to get a competitive edge, and we are always looking for ways to spend money on high-tech gadgets. One of the most stylish and useful is a digital thermometer that has a central unit that connects to one or two probes. The probes are inserted into the thickest portion of the meat and give you a live digital readout of what's going on inside. This is a godsend because when you poke an instant-read thermometer into meat and remove it, you create a hole that allows the precious juices to run out. The probe-style devices avoid this because the thermometer stays in the meat for the entire cooking time.

Tennessee whiskey: See cribbage board and card table.

Trouble light: Handy for illuminating barbecue equipment and card games in the middle of the night.

Vinyl gloves: Keep a box of these disposable gloves on hand at all times. This is a huge convenience in competition, and it also enhances hygiene when you're dealing with raw meat.

To Newberg ... and Glory!
How Barbecue Changed My Life

Chapter II

s Vince, Tom and I barrelled south on the I-5, on our way to Oregon, the mood was buoyant. We were loaded for bear... and ready to cook barbecue. The van was crammed with coolers full of meat and booze, plus the whole whack of paraphernalia that usually accompanies us to competitions, including our collection of knives, cutting boards, barbecue rubs, sauces, marinades, charcoal, hardwood chips and chunks, electronic thermometers, tables and patio furniture.

The van smelled of smoke from the four Weber bullets stacked in the back. For amateur competitors like us, the bullets—called Smokey Mountain Cookers by their manufacturer, but nicknamed bullets for their black, oblong design—are the cooker of choice. On any given day, meat cooked in these cheap, well-designed and reliable babies can beat whatever the bigtime pitmasters can cook in their giant $10,000 dual-wheeled rigs.

We left Vancouver at 10 a.m. after picking up the pork butts at Penguin Meats near the Canada / U.S. border in White Rock. The butts were perfect nine-pounders, bone in, with creamy white fat caps. We tossed them in the cooler along with the four racks of side ribs, three free-range organic chickens and two of the best triple A briskets I'd ever seen, each weighing in at about 12 lbs. / 5.5 kg and costing about sixty bucks each.

By 11 o'clock we had reached the Peace Arch border crossing on our way to Newberg, Oregon, the small, rural bedroom community outside of Portland where the big contest was being held. As we pulled away from the border, young Tom yelled what would become the Butt Shredders' rallying cry.

"To Newberg... and GLORY!" he shouted, and we couldn't stop laughing. Tom's exclamation had just the right combination of bravado and pomposity for a barbecue team. It also captured the mood of the moment. We felt like an invading army, going deep into alien territory to fight a historic battle on the adversary's home turf. The Oregon State Open was the Pacific Northwest's oldest barbecue championship, and some of the best of the best would be gathering in the storage yard behind the

Newberg Ace Hardware, including several state and regional champions. As a Kansas City Barbecue Society (KCBS)-sanctioned event, the Oregon Open would attract everyone in the Pacific Northwest who wanted to take a crack at qualifying for The Royal and The Jack.

꒰ ꒱

Earlier that year I had lost my job as a PR executive. Licking my wounds but armed with a severance package, I began the search for another corporate job, but the pickings were slim. The economy was in the toilet and no one was hiring. Knowing things would not pick up until at least the fall, I applied myself to enjoying the summer with my family. We live in lush, green North Vancouver, British Columbia, one of the most beautiful places on earth, in the middle of the coastal rain forest. It would be a healing summer of picnics on the beach, long walks with the dog and mountain biking in the forest.

Not to mention barbecue. The hiatus from work also allowed me to focus on my favorite pastime. With a group of old friends I had been entering barbecue contests for seven years, but so far Rockin' Ronnie's Butt Shredders had not seen a victory. Our performance had improved over the years, but in recent contests the Butt Shredders had become barbecue bridesmaids, winning in some categories but consistently placing second overall or, in the overblown barbecue-speak of the competition circuit, finishing as Reserve Grand Champions. With time on my hands and a smoldering passion to win a barbecue contest, I looked forward to the coming season with high hopes.

The plan for 2001 was to take the Canadian Championship in Vancouver by storm in August and keep the momentum going at Barbecue on the Bow in Calgary on the Labour Day weekend.

As the summer progressed there was bad news. The founder of the Canadian Barbecue Championship and Canada's best-known promoter of real barbecue, David "The Fire Chef" Valjacic, was dying of cancer and the big contest was cancelled for that year. Our plans of making a stand at "the Canadians" were off and Labour Day was a long way off.

Around the same time that I found out about

the cancellation, the latest edition of *Drippings from the Pit*, the official newsletter of the Pacific Northwest Barbecue Association, arrived in the mail. Among reports on the latest Spring Training barbecue workshops in Washington State and box scores on the results of recent contests, there was a flyer promoting the Oregon State Open Barbecue Championship.

Yes. That's it, I thought. The Butt Shredders had never competed in a U.S. championship before, and the Oregon Open was a qualifier for the American Royal in Kansas City—the World Series of Barbecue—and the Jack Daniel's Invitational World Championship, the Holy Grail of competitive barbecue.

It was time to take a stab at The Big Meat.

⤚ ⤛

After the first couple of hours fighting the Friday afternoon Seattle-area traffic, it was pretty smooth sailing the rest of the way down to Portland, with stops at roadside diners along the way for cheeseburgers and cherry pie, washed down with hot black coffee. Vince, our map man, had downloaded complete travel directions from the Web and we wended our way through the back roads outside of Portland, pulling into Ace Hardware around seven that night.

We were among the last ones to get to the competition grounds. Most of the teams already had their briskets and pork butts on, while we hurried to set up. Organizer of the contest Mark Vergets treated us like visiting royalty. We were the only Canadians to ever drive that far south in the 14-year history of the contest. Mark had an awning set up for us when we arrived, with a power hook-up all set to go. Sixteen other teams had registered for the contest, including at least four winners of other recent competitions.

After about half an hour of scrambling to unload and do a quick-and-dirty setup, we hooked up our lights and hauled the briskets out of the cooler. With brisket turn-in to the judges only 15 hours away, we had no time to lose. The briskets were big, and should have been in the cooker hours ago.

Working with my filleting knife, I trimmed the fat caps on the two briskets down to the ideal 1/8-inch/3-mm thickness. Tom, whose father is a surgeon, is our best rub man. He can sprinkle rub on a brisket like a detailer in an auto-body shop working with an airbrush on a vintage Chevy.

Working together, we painted the briskets with mustard, applied a light sprinkle of granulated garlic and hit them with a heavy coating of rub. In the meantime Vince got the bullets set up, filled the charcoal baskets with briquettes and started the fires in the two cookers that would hold the briskets and pork butts. It was a race against time.

By 9 o'clock the briskets and pork butts were in the smokers and we could relax a bit and start prepping the ribs and chicken. Other competitors whom we knew from previous contests drifted over to say hello, beers were cracked open and I uncorked a bottle of Oregon Sauvignon Blanc we picked up at a Fred Meyer megastore on the way into town. We had walked around the huge Fred Meyer in awe, unaccustomed to giant box stores like this. We still buy our wine at the B.C. Liquor Control Board, and we don't have supermarkets with a produce department and a liquor store that also sells tires and barbecue equipment.

As the evening rolled on we started to get into the rhythm of what barbecue contests are all about. We were happy. We had abandoned our daily lives and become citizens of Barbecueville, a temporary tent city that needs no laws but the rules of judging set out by the Kansas City Barbecue Society. The main industry in Barbecueville is a mild form of debauchery that involves drinking, cooking, eating meat and staying up all night listening to Waylon Jennings's greatest hits, as hickory smoke wafts across a skyline glittering with chili-shaped patio lights. Throughout the year our chubby nomadic tribe moves from contest to contest, building and then taking down our ramshackle city as if it were a three-ring circus.

We had abandoned our daily lives and become citizens of Barbecueville.

We call what we do a championship, but it's the only competition where the event and the tailgate party are exactly the same thing. Even so-called sports like curling and darts don't count cribbage boards as standard equipment. And even though we're all "competing," what we're really doing is what we love—cooking and eating barbecue. Once you have had one aromatic, succulent, deeply satisfying bite of real barbecue, fresh out of the cooker, your life has permanently changed. To taste a perfectly cooked slice of brisket, or to experience the texture of pulled pork, piled high on a fluffy white bun, drizzled with vinegary sauce and topped with crunchy, sweet coleslaw, or to bite into a rib and feel the tender meat come gently off the bone as you taste the tangy, salty, sweet, savory pork, is just one step short of heaven. And when you can claim that you not only cook barbecue, but cook the best barbecue, you are not just a winner but a culinary demi-god, bringing a greasy nirvana within reach of those around you.

≽ ≼

I had no idea of what I was getting into in the summer of 1994, when my old friend Rocco Ciancio invited me over to his ranch on the outskirts of Calgary to show me the new water smoker he had bought on a recent trip to Texas. He and his wife, Denise, had been down to attend a relative's wedding in San Antonio. Rocco was amazed and charmed by the topic of most conversations between Texans: the quality of the brisket they had barbecued over the weekend. Before he left, Rocco visited a Costco and for US$20 got himself a cheap Brinkman water smoker. When he got home he bought a couple of books on home smoking and, from then on, his weekends were spent experimenting with his new toy, smoking sausages, ducks, chickens and testing out exotic recipes for things like smoked Peruvian lamb hearts.

He invited me to join in the fun, and before long we were calling his house Rocky's Smokehouse and Commercial Sausage Upgrader. Before long I got another friend, the local restaurant critic Kathy Richardier, interested in smoking food. She and I went halfers on an electric smoker and it just kind of took off from there. But back then we were interested in smoking food and didn't even really know what true barbecue was.

In the spring of 1996 our barbecue journey began in earnest, when Kathy and I and a few other foodie friends joined a group of Calgary cooks for

an all-day workshop on championship barbecue. Bob Lyon, the granddaddy of barbecue in the Pacific Northwest and president of the Pacific Northwest Barbecue Association, came up to Calgary from his home base in Washington State to show us Canucks a thing or two about how to cook barbecue for competition. Bob came to town at the request of Carol and Sandy Dougall, organizers of Calgary's Barbecue on the Bow. The contest was entering its third year and gaining in popularity, but Carol and Sandy were dismayed that the vast majority of the competitors were U.S.-based teams. They loved hosting the out-of-towners, but they didn't like the fact that the Americans went back with all the shiny hardware every year. By bringing Bob in, they planned to raise the interest and skill level among Calgary barbecue cooks in hopes of increasing the number of Canadian teams—and improving their chances of winning.

Bob, a white-haired, erudite 70-something, was editor of *Drippings from the Pit*, chief cook of the Beaver Castors (named "Barbecue Road Team of the 90s"), and a seasoned veteran of The Royal and The Jack. He spent the day sharing his knowledge with us and coaching us as we cooked ribs and chicken on our cheap charcoal-fueled covered grills and water smokers. At the end of the day Bob even staged a little contest, showing us how to carve and present our barbecue in competition and giving us a chance to judge each other's cooking according to the KCBS rules.

Shortly after, Rockin' Ronnie's Butt Shredders was formed, and in September we entered our first competition. We won Best New Cooks at Barbecue on the Bow that year, but more importantly, we were on our way to becoming indoctrinated in the culture, values and mores of Barbecueville.

I had a great team, which spread over two cities after my job took me to Vancouver. In Calgary, my hometown, the core team was Kathy, Rocco and Ann-Marie ("Amo") Jackson, a great cook who had learned to love barbecue while living in Texas in the 1980s. And in Vancouver, I had convinced long-time friends Stephen Robertson and Vince Gogolek and Tom Masterson, the 15-year-old son of my cousin Paula, to be the West Coast contingent of the Butt Shredders.

The two Canadian competitions we entered

every year—Barbecue on the Bow in Calgary and the Canadian Championship in Vancouver, British Columbia, were always stacked with ringers. Successful American teams like Sum Say, Mad Momma & the Kids, the Beaver Castors, Smokestack Lightnin' and the Doughboys would come up to Canada because the events were smaller and the few Canadian teams that entered were inexperienced. Winning the Canadian events, which were sanctioned by the the Kansas City Barbecue Society, earned the victors an invitation to the big season-ending contests. So, for many teams in the Pacific Northwest, the long drive to Canada was more than an exotic location. It was a better chance than any to earn a spot at The Royal and The Jack.

There was a lot to learn from the American teams. Each year, as we drifted around the competition grounds, jawing with our fellow competitors, we would pick up a few tips and meet a few more characters. People like the Dakota Kid, known outside of Barbecueville as Harold Froescher, a veteran barbecue competitor whose claim to fame was a perfect 180 score on his ribs at the American Royal in 1994.

The first time I saw Dakota was at Barbecue on the Bow in '97. It was ten o'clock in the evening, and we had the usual cool Canadian autumn weather. You could see your breath that night. He had a makeshift rig—a homemade Rube Goldberg contraption that combined a sleeping compartment with a rolling barbecue pit, including a fold-out awning and built-in cupboards for all his tools. I came up to him from behind as he hunched over a scrawny pork butt with a fillet knife, muttering to himself. Despite the cold he was sweating. With his ratty sleeveless undershirt and head-mounted flashlight, he looked like a deranged surgeon—a squat, scowling, bowling ball of a man who clearly had some regrets about making the trip to Calgary. After introducing myself I asked him if there was something wrong.

"You can't get a decent pork butt in this town," Dakota grumbled. "The meat up here in Canada is way too lean. Look at this butt. All the fat's been trimmed out of it. How the hell am I supposed to cook this thing?"

I laughed and gave him a friendly, man-style

shoulder hug. His big, clammy arms were cold with sweat.

He started to warm up, at least conversation-wise. "'Course nowadays you don't know what the judges want anyway. They don't like seein' any fat at all on your meat." He frowned. "That's stupid. Brisket's gotta have some fat on it to cook right." To get around this, Dakota showed me how he trimmed all the fat off his briskets and then laid strips of it on the meat, moving them to the top every time he turned the brisket over.

A couple of years later I ran into Dakota at the Canadian championships. He was as sad and grumpy as ever, so big that he shambled along like a Grizzly bear and wore leather moccasins for comfort. A proud barbecue champion, he spoke with a tinge of anger and resentment about being shut out of the prize money for several contests in a row. He was thinking of giving it up, throwing in the tongs after this year. I asked him what he thought his chances were in tomorrow's judging.

There was a lot to learn from the American teams.

"I dunno. I just don't know any more," he said, hanging his head. "I'm usin' some hickory, some apple, some mesquite. I got the garlic granules. But I just don't know." I first learned about garlic granules from Dakota, a secret trick that makes the judges' taste buds stand at attention as soon as they bite into your barbecue.

The Dakota Kid would take it all the next day, winning the Grand Champion title and buying himself yet another ticket to the American Royal. He was beaming as he trundled up to get his trophy.

≻ ≺

As dawn broke on judging day of the 2001 Oregon Open, all hell broke loose in our makeshift field kitchen in the back of Ace Hardware. I'd grabbed a couple hours of sleep in our nearby motel room. Hungover from living the barbecue lifestyle the night before, I took a shower, left Vince to sleep for a while longer and headed back down to our tent. It was 7 a.m. The sky was gray and the parking lot was damp from rain during the night.

Tom, who had taken the graveyard shift to tend the cookers, was fast asleep in a folding chair. When I arrived I took a quick glance around and saw that the chamber temperature on the brisket was down to 140. We had ourselves a situation.

"Tom! Wake up! The briskets have lost temperature!"

Tom rubbed his eyes. "What's the internal?"

"It's down to 140. And the meat's only at 135!"

"I don't know what happened, Rockin'…when I closed my eyes an hour ago it was holding steady at test!"

This was bad. Even in ideal conditions at 212 degrees, it was touch-and-go whether we'd have enough time to get the briskets done before turn-in at eleven. The probe inside the brisket gave us a reading that showed we were at 130—a full 40 degrees short of a finished product. Thankfully, the pork butts were holding steady, but the cold, rainy night had taken its toll on the briskets. The pit masters with the big rolling barbecue rigs never had this problem with their huge fireboxes and giant heat-retaining mass.

With only two hours to go before turn-in time we decided to take drastic measures.

We opened the vents on the distressed smoker and quickly worked to get a couple of chimneys of hot coals going. There is nothing worse than rubbery, undercooked brisket. We had to get the internal temperature up to at least 170 as soon as possible so the proteins and connective tissue in the brisket would break down, creating the succulent texture of classic barbecue.

In the meantime the pork butt was doing fine, with the temperature coming up nicely. It was already at 150 and we would take the butts out of the cooker when they reached 165 degrees. With three hours to go before turn-in, there was still plenty of time. Tom worked to replenish the coals under the briskets and butts.

Vince soon arrived and quickly got to work doing his final prep on the ribs, removing the membrane and coating them with mustard and rub. I butchered the chickens, taking care to keep their precious fat-giving skin intact, and got them into the marinade.

By 10 o'clock the internal temperature of the brisket had gone up to 160 or so. Still not high enough to cook properly. With only two hours to go before turn-in time we decided to take drastic measures. We took the water pan out from under the briskets, then wrapped each piece of meat in a thick coating of heavy foil and placed them back in the smoker. Now we needed a quick source of heat, and briquettes would take a good 20 minutes to start up.

I decided to use most of our remaining dry cherry wood chunks to make some natural charcoal, which would burn hotter and faster than briquettes. The goal was to build a healthy fire under the briskets, pushing the chamber temperature to nearly 400 degrees. Our only hope was that the high heat would somehow pressure-cook the foil-wrapped briskets and get them tender enough in time for turn-in.

Paying all that attention to the brisket made us take our eyes off the ribs, which were losing temperature in the cool of the morning. They weren't in as much danger as the briskets, but they definitely needed tending. Suddenly it looked like we might screw up both the ribs and the briskets. At the same time, the coals for the chicken were almost ready.

Again, we had to act quickly. After some frantic discussion we agreed on a course of action. One of the advantages of the Weber bullets is their interchangeability. The modular design allows for the body of the smoker to be removed without disturbing the charcoal basket underneath. We would take the chamber containing the ribs and switch it with the one that the chicken was about to go in, which was full of fresh hot coals. We needed heat on the ribs immediately, and chicken, which is easy to overcook, would be fine in a cooler chamber with half-spent coals.

All three of us went into action. From a distance it must have looked like a strange, frantic dance, with three men staggering around in oven mitts, switching smoking chambers and yelling instructions at one another.

It was chaos on one level. But, on another, we were playing at the peak of our game. Like a pro golfer who gets caught in the rough, we were drawing on everything we knew to get out of a bad

situation. With a foundation of seven years of competitions under our belt, we were at a skill level where we could improvise in response to a crisis. Although what we were attempting looked crazy, we were actually working very hard to keep things under control.

Or so we thought. A few minutes after our little dance I took a quick peek under the lid of one of the smokers, which I thought contained the ribs. But it was the briskets! That meant the ribs were in a 400-degree smoker. Way too hot. And our briskets were languishing in the smoker right next to it.

I felt like an idiot. Like out-of-town rubes drawn into a bizarre shell game, we had lost track of which meat was in which cooker!

More shouting. More stumbling about. More shuffling of equipment. Finally, everything was where it was supposed to be, with only an hour before the first turn-in. Exhausted but full of adrenalin, we put the chicken on and gave the pork butt its final glaze before wrapping it in foil to rest before we carved it for the judges. The ribs were doing fine and the briskets, still wrapped in foil, were steaming away in the chamber above the hot cherry wood coals.

Somewhere in the middle of that chaos, I was tending one of the bullets when I heard a familiar voice.

"How ya doin', boys?" It was Harold Froescher.

"The Dakota Kid!" I gasped, jumping up to shake his hand. "We didn't see you last night. Are you competing?" He laughed as he shambled into our enclosure.

"Nope. I'm semi-retired. Got the diabetes, and it's slowin' me down. I got some friends who have a team here. I'm just hangin' around and givin' 'em advice, whether they want it or not!"

"Got any advice for us, Dakota? How do you think we're going to do?"

He looked at me, smiled, laid his big, meaty hand on my shoulder, and said, "Son, there's a lot of good cooks here today. But I wish you the best of luck." With that he turned and trundled on back to his buddies.

⌇ ⌇

The Kansas City Barbecue Society sets out strict rules for the presentation and judging of barbecue. There are four, and only four, official categories in a KCBS-sanctioned event: brisket, pork shoulder (whole or Boston butt), ribs and chicken. Only green leaf lettuce can be used as a bed for the meat, and only parsley or cilantro can be used as garnish.

Every contestant gets 4 white, hinged Styrofoam take-out trays, each with a standard door prize–style double ticket taped to the bottom. You tear off one of the tickets when you get your containers and leave the duplicate tickets taped to the container. That way no one knows which team cooked what—until they announce the numbers of the winning contestants for each category. Entries must be turned in within 5 minutes of the official turn-in times, which are usually an hour apart, starting at 11 a.m. with brisket, then pork shoulder, then chicken, then ribs. Each entry is scored by 6 judges, on a scale of 1 to 9, on three criteria: appearance, texture and taste. The taste score is doubled and the lowest score on each criterion is thrown out.

The taste score is doubled in recognition of the fact that taste is the most important component of great barbecue. But barbecue competitors know that the judges eat first with their eyes. If your presentation looks mouth-wateringly good, it will simply taste better.

In addition to my role as team captain, I'm the knife man, taking the lead in putting together the presentation of each entry. The trick is to find ways to present 6 or more pieces of meat on a bed of leaf lettuce that makes the judges want to jump right into the container.

⌇ ⌇

We were on that morning in Newberg. When I took the briskets out of the foil they were a bit charred on the bottoms from being directly above the fire with a dry water pan, but otherwise they were perfectly juicy and tender. The 6 slices of brisket we presented, with their thin layer of tasty fat and bright red smoke ring, looked positively succulent. The pork butts were smoked to a glistening mahogany perfection and we arranged them on the lettuce in our usual style: 6 half-inch medallions taken from the richest part of the butt and laid neatly across the container diagonally, with a heaping pile of lightly sauced and shredded meat on either side.

The chicken pieces, which had been brined, basted and sauced meticulously by Vince and Tom, were gloriously shiny and dotted with little bits of parsley as they came out of the cooker. The 6 beautiful white slices of breast meat seemed to fall into place in the presentation tray, nestled between a plump leg–thigh combo and a golden brown wing. A small sprig of parsley was all it took to finish it off. It looked like something out of a magazine.

With each successive turn-in we were more confident—except for the ribs, our Achilles heel. In all our years of competition we had never placed better than sixth in ribs. The tiny, lean racks available in fat-conscious Canada didn't help. Our ribs always seemed to come out dry and overcooked, or tough and undercooked. They didn't have a distinctive flavor, and because we knew they were a problem, we always over-fussed them, often coating them with too much sauce and drowning out the flavor of the pork. Our turn-in looked only okay. But what the hell, we thought. No one's perfect.

One of the most important parts of barbecue competitions is the post-mortem—the team discussion of what went wrong and what went right as we go over our scores and second-guess the judges. This dialogue begins during the hour and a half after the last turn-in, while the judges' marks are being compiled. As we started breaking down our little camp, dumping our coals and drippings, scouring the grills and putting away our tools, we talked about how it had gone, and it had clearly gone pretty well. But as the ritual of announcing the winners began and the head judge called the numbers, in ascending order from tenth to first place, we were stunned.

We won brisket. Then pork shoulder ... and then chicken. By the time ribs were being announced (we didn't even crack the top 10) it didn't matter because it wasn't a contest anymore. On that day in

Newberg, the Butt Shredders became the first Canadian team ever to win the Oregon Open, and, in fact, the first Canadians to win any U.S. barbecue competition, ever.

Adding to the prestige and glamor of the occasion, our big shiny plastic trophies were handed to us by the beautiful Queen of Newberg's Old Fashioned Days and her two smiling Courtiers. They were pretty country girls dressed in strapless pink taffeta gowns, replete with classic white beauty-queen sashes.

We made it. We had finally achieved barbecue glory. And in the process we had learned some barbecue secrets—about how to cook and present our meat, and, even more importantly, about how high each of us could reach, and how much our team could achieve. A great, great feeling.

Minutes after we walked away from the judging area, I called my wife, Kate, on my cell phone. "Mama, git yerself a new pair of shoes! We're goin' to Kansas City! Woo hoo!"

The seven-hour trip back to Vancouver seemed to go by in about two blinks. Its highlight was going through the border crossing. The unsuspecting guard asked the usual questions.

"Do you have anything to declare?" she asked, looking at our passports.

"Yes," said Vince. "I declare we're the winners of the Oregon State Open Barbecue Championship!"

Or that's how I remember it. Vince and Tom say it was more like, "Why were you visiting the U.S.?" "We competed in a barbecue contest." "Did you win?" "Yes, we did!" But part of barbecue culture is embellishing stories and I like my version better.

All the way back to Vancouver we replayed the entire contest, going over the moves we'd made, celebrating every moment, and laughing at the crazy path we had taken to victory that morning. Our little voodoo dance with the bullets had worked.

On Sunday morning, I put out a news release to local Vancouver media and on Monday there was a color photo of our team at the top of page 3 of the *Vancouver Sun* with the headline: SIZZLING BUTT SHREDDERS WIN U.S. BARBECUE OPEN and a quote from me saying the event was "a pure meat experience." That afternoon I was interviewed by the Canadian Broadcasting Corporation for a show that aired across B.C. The owners of the local NHL team, the Vancouver Canucks, sent us a congratulatory note and some free hockey tickets for the team.

But more glorious than anything else was the berth we had earned at the American Royal Invitational that October in Kansas City. Six of us would travel down to the U.S. that fall to compete in The Royal. But that's a whole other story.

⊱ EPILOGUE ⊰

So, how did barbecue change my life? Some hard work, some laughs, a hangover, a few gaudy plastic trophies, a picture in the paper and some free hockey tickets do not constitute a profound change in anyone's existence.

But when the Dakota Kid put his hand on my shoulder, I had a barbecue epiphany. I realized that barbecue competitions, and barbecue culture, are not just a goofy sport, and that they are more than a lifestyle. Barbecue, I realized, is a metaphor for life itself. It's a fat, juicy prism through which we can look at the human condition.

I don't know about you, but I find it hard to get a whole lot of personal fulfilment working in the corporate world. Hamstrung by bureaucracy, stifled by bad internal politics, frustrated by the Kafkaesque absurdity of life in the modern workplace, I am drawn to barbecue for its purity, its simple meaning, and a true feeling of joy that brings me to a happier place. The smokey cocoon of the barbecue contest creates a relaxed, friendly community unlike anything in urban life today.

Being on a barbecue team gives its members a sense of purpose and camaraderie that's hard to find anywhere else. And being the chief cook of a barbecue team has given me a chance to be a leader, making decisions, solving problems, coaching and collaborating with teammates, delegating responsibility, bickering when things go wrong, and sharing in the glory when we win.

Finally, I think it's fair to say that our victory on that fateful day in Oregon has led to this book. Being a barbecue champion has given me a unique little niche in an increasingly generic world. It has opened doors that I never knew existed, strengthened my old friendships and introduced me to new ones. And it has given me a chance to cook, and eat, the most delicious food on earth.

Barbecue has made me whole. God bless barbecue.

5. The final temperature of your meat is more important than how long you cook it. Watch the internal temperature of your meat and you will produce great barbecue, time after time.

6. Let it rest. Resting your meat after you take it off the heat allows the juices to redistribute inside within the protective crust. It also allows the protein to set, or gel, almost like a custard. Resting lets the meat come to the perfect texture.

7. Sauce lightly, or don't sauce at all. The tang of a barbecue sauce (called a finishing glaze in barbecue circles) helps to complete the perfect barbecue flavor. But it can also overpower the flavor of barbecue, so you don't taste much else but the sauce. Go lightly, and then serve some "dipping sauce" on the side.

8. Use a combo of woods for complex flavor. Use hardwood as a flavoring agent, but learn what combination works for you. Just like a blended whisky provides the taster with different flavor notes, some sharp, some sweet, hardwood can be just as subtle. Use mesquite for astringent sharpness, fruitwood for rich sweetness, and hickory, maple and oak for classic barbecue flavor.

A SELECTION OF MENUS

Championship Barbecue Feast

There's a reason most of these recipes have the word "classic" in them. Serve your favorite summer beverages like cold beer and Jack Daniel's and Coke.

Classic North Carolina Barbecued Pulled Pork Sandwiches (page 126)

North Carolina–Style Vinegar Sauce (page 66)

Classic Mustard-Based Barbecue Sauce (page 67)

Tidewater Coleslaw (page 100)

Classic Baked Beans for a Crowd (page 88)

Classic Lemon Meringue Pie (page 186)

Serves 15 to 20 if you're cooking two butts

Asian-Themed Barbecue Supper

A hot summer night, some good friends, and delicious Asian flavors. What could be better? Serve cold Asian beer like Kirin, Tsing-Tao or Kingfisher and a nice crisp, fruity Riesling or Sauvignon Blanc.

Prosciutto-Wrapped Prawn and Lychee Kebabs (page 170)

Kate's Tasty Asian Chicken Thighs (page 138)

Asian Noodle Salad with Sesame Mayonnaise (page 105)

Grilled Asparagus (page 74)

Ginger Cake with Lemon Sauce (page 184)

Serves 4 to 6

Southwestern Heat

I would recommend starting out this evening with a round or two of Rocky Mountain Margaritas (page 199) and then moving to Mexican beer and/or a big chewy red wine like a Shiraz.

Funky Quesadillas (page 71) and Fiery Southwestern Wings (page 142)

Smoked Tomato Guacamole (page 79)

Chipotle and Roasted Garlic Aïoli (page 73)

Flank Steak Fajitas Adobo with Mango Strawberry Salsa (page 154)

Latin–Style Rice and Black Beans (page 99)

Grilled Pineapple with Caramel Sauce (page 194)

Serves 4 to 6

Mediterranean Flavors

This menu requires a little fussing, what with the grilling of all the vegetables and the stuffing of the burgers and the prep for the ratatouille, but the end result is a tasty and casual meal. Serve the ratatouille as a side or a condiment. I would serve Greek retsina (a resiny white wine) with this for those with adventurous palates, but any hearty red and/or full-bodied white will do just fine.

Grilled Little Fish (page 169)

Grilled Vegetable Platter (half recipe) (page 74)

Lamb Burger with Molten Goat Cheese Core (page 120)

Ratatouille (page 87)

Applesauce Cake with Penuche Icing (page 190)

Serves 4

A Super-Easy Family Dinner

It's Friday night, the kids are home and everyone needs an end-of-week lift. This easy but very satisfying menu will start the weekend on the right foot. It's also great for last-minute entertaining. Use a savory butter for the corn if you've got it but in a pinch, butter and kosher salt will do. Serve with iced tea or Coke for the kids, cold beer or a nice Cabernet Sauvignon for the adults.

Easiest Ever Appetizer (page 72)

Supercharged Corn on the Cob (with plain or savory butter) (page 90)

Easiest, Tastiest Steak (page 146)

Field Greens with Walnut Oil and Toasted Pumpkin Seeds (page 102)

The Ultimate Triple-Chocolate Brownies (page 180) with vanilla ice cream

9. Barbecue is about balance. Balance your flavors to create a single, complex but unified taste. Balance your temperature, length of cooking time and resting time to achieve the perfect texture. Balance the appearance of the barbecue on your guest's plate or the judges' tray, so your portion looks plentiful but not vulgar, and moist but not oversauced, richly luxurious, but with some fresh green as a visual counterpoint.

10. Barbecue is life. Good food and drink, friendship, humor, healthy competition—that's what barbecue and life are all about. As an old boss of mine once said, "Ronnie, if you use people good, they'll use you good." Be gentle with your barbecue and with your friends, and you shall lead a wonderful life.

A Selection of Rubs, Marinades and Sauces
pages 49 to 68

Prosciutto-wrapped Prawn and Lychee Kebabs
page 170

Lamb Kebabs with Dilled Lemony Rice
pages 157 and 94

Quesadillas served with Smoked Tomato Guacamole
pages 70 to 71, 79

Rubs, Marinades and Sauces

Chapter III

RUBS

Chef Paul Kirk, the Baron of Barbecue and multiple World Champion, says if there's one single factor that most influences the taste of barbecue, it's the rub. Every barbecue competitor has his or her secret recipe, but pretty much every barbecue rub has 3 essential components: salt, sugar and spices, usually dominated by onion, garlic and chile flavors. Even though you may never have tasted real Southern-style barbecue, everyone in North America has experienced the classic taste of barbecue rub in the sweet, tangy coating of your favorite brand of barbecue potato chips or in the store-bought seasoning salt you sprinkle on your steaks and burgers.

The ideal barbecue rub should be balanced, with a rich, blended flavor that sparkles on your tongue like biting into a ripe cherry tomato. And it should have an aftertaste, like a good port or scotch, lingering in the mouth and resonating like a tuning fork. Finally, it should have some heat, with a sharpness at the beginning and a long, gentle, satisfying burn that stays on your palate and prompts you to want more.

The longer rubs stand after you mix them, the richer and more balanced the flavor. Try to store a batch of rub for at least a few days before using it. Well-sealed and stored in a cool, dry cupboard, rubs keep for at least 6 months. The first 3 rub recipes in this section can be modified to suit the meat you're smoking and your personal taste. Add powdered ginger and some five-spice powder for an Asian touch; cumin, powdered oregano and coriander for a Southwestern flavor; powdered sage to enhance pork; or allspice, nutmeg and cloves for an old-world European flavor. It's best not to add more than 3 extra herbs or spices to a classic barbecue rub; any more than that and you've got too much going on and the flavor will not feel true.

championship BARBECUE RUB (a.k.a. bob's rub)

makes about 3 cups | 750 mL

The Butt Shredders call this Bob's Rub, and it's what we use in competition. Bob Lyon, the grand-daddy of barbecue in the Pacific Northwest, shared this at a barbecue workshop that first introduced me to the joys of real barbecue and prompted me to become a barbecue competitor. It follows a rule of thumb that's worth remembering: a third, a third, a third. Which means one-third sugar, one-third seasoned salts, and one-third dry herbs and spices.

1 cup | 250 mL white sugar

1/4 cup | 50 mL celery salt

1/4 cup | 50 mL garlic salt

1/4 cup | 50 mL onion salt

1/4 cup | 50 mL seasoning salt (I like Lawrey's)

1/3 cup | 75 mL chili powder (use a commercial blend, or if you want an edge, try a combination of real ground chiles like ancho, poblano, New Mexico or guahilla)

1/3 cup | 75 mL black pepper

1/3 cup | 75 mL paprika

To this basic rub add as much heat as you want, using cayenne pepper, hot paprika or ground chipotles. Then add 2 or 3 signature spices to suit whatever you're cooking or your personal taste, like powdered thyme, oregano, cumin, sage, powdered ginger, etc. Add only 1 to 3 tsp. / 5 to 15 mL of each signature seasoning so as not to overpower the rub.

TEXAS style RUB

makes about 2 cups | 500 mL

Everyone has a friend of a friend of a friend who knows someone in Texas with a great rub recipe. This one came to me through occasional Butt Shredder and barbecue enthusiast Ian "Big Daddy" Baird. The cayenne gives it a nice burn. Use it as an all-purpose rub, but it really makes brisket sing (see the King of Barbecue: Beef Brisket, page 150).

3/4 cup | 175 mL paprika

1/4 cup | 50 mL kosher salt

1/4 cup | 50 mL sugar

1/4 cup | 50 mL ground black pepper

1/4 cup | 50 mL chile powder

2 Tbsp. | 25 mL garlic powder

2 Tbsp. | 25 mL onion powder

1 Tbsp. | 15 mL cayenne, or to taste

Combine all ingredients well.

ROCKIN' RONNIE'S GRILLING rub

Makes about 1 cup | 250 mL

I like to use this combination of seasonings for everyday grilling (grilling rubs contain little or no sugar because the higher heat of grilling would make a sugary rub turn black). It perfectly balances the earthiness of the toasted cumin, the sharpness of ground pepper, the smokiness and heat of the ground chipotles and the natural sweetness of the ancho chile, granulated onion and garlic.

4 Tbsp. | 60 mL kosher salt

1 tsp. | 5 mL ground pepper

2 Tbsp. | 25 mL ground toasted cumin seeds

1 Tbsp. | 15 mL ground oregano

2 Tbsp. | 25 mL granulated onion

1 Tbsp. | 15 mL granulated garlic

2 Tbsp. | 25 mL ancho chile powder

1 tsp. | 5 mL ground chipotles
(if you can't find this substitute cayenne)

1 tsp. | 5 mL dried parsley

Combine all the ingredients well.

mediterranean dried HERB RUB

These days food lovers tend to shy away from dried herbs in favor of the fresh ones that are so readily available. We tend to associate unpleasantly stale, dirty flavors with dried herbs, but that's probably because we use them so rarely that the ones in our pantry are too old. Dried herbs, when used within a few months of purchasing them, can add a wonderful earthiness and complexity to grilled foods. In fact, the high heat of grilling often destroys the delicate flavors of fresh herbs. In most cases fresh herbs, other than the very strong rosemary and sage, are best used after your meat is off the grill, as a finely chopped sprinkle to add color and aroma. Use this rub for meats like chicken and pork, but it also works well with grilled vegtables. Just toss the veggies with oil and sprinkle with the rub and some kosher salt.

1 Tbsp.| 15 mL dried (not powdered) oregano

1 Tbsp.| 15 mL dried mint

1 Tbsp.| 15 mL dried basil

1 Tbsp.| 15 mL dried rosemary

1 tsp.| 5 mL dried parsley

Combine all ingredients well.

old RUB
WORLD

Makes about 1/2 cup | 125 mL

Smell this rub to conjure up images of holiday roasts, mulled wine and spice cake. Use it on leaner cuts of pork tenderloin or rib roast.

1/4 cup | 50 mL white sugar

1/4 cup | 50 mL kosher salt

1 tsp. | 5 mL freshly grated nutmeg (about half a nut)

2 tsp. | 10 mL ground cinnamon

2 tsp. | 10 mL ground allspice

1 tsp. | 5 mL powdered basil or thyme

1/4 tsp. | 1 mL ground cloves

Combine all ingredients well.

60s Retro Rub

In the 1950s the Culinary Arts Institute of Chicago published *The Master Chef's Outdoor Grill Cookbook*, which featured delicious recipes like Ground Meat in Barbecue Sauce, Bacon Steaks and my personal favorite, Barbecued Bologna Roll ("Quick and easy. Inexpensive. Good!") This is the book's featured barbecue rub for charcoal-broiled steak.

1 Tbsp. | 15 mL salt

2 tsp. | 10 mL monosodium glutamate

1/4 tsp. | 1 mL freshly ground pepper

Wow, did they go wild on the pepper! Now if that's not repressed, I don't know what is. Those were the days, indeed.

mediterranean MARINADE

Makes enough for a couple of racks of lamb, four chicken breasts or eight chicken thighs

Don't let the anchovy scare you. It adds a wonderful depth of flavor and the end product doesn't taste fishy at all.

1/2 cup | 125 mL extra virgin olive oil

1 Tbsp. | 15 mL Dijon mustard

**1 Tbsp. | 15 mL olive paste or 6 calamata olives,
pitted and chopped**

1 anchovy fillet

1 Tbsp. | 15 mL coarsely chopped fresh rosemary

1 Tbsp. | 15 mL chopped fresh basil

1 Tbsp. | 15 mL chopped fresh mint

1 Tbsp. | 15 mL Mediterranean Dried Herb Rub (see page 54)

juice of 1 lemon

1 Tbsp. | 15 mL balsamic vinegar

Combine all ingredients in a food processor and whiz until blended but not totally puréed.

MARINADES

Marinades add a lovely layer of complexity to the flavor of grilled or barbecued meats. Research has shown that acidic marinades tend to neutralize the carcinogenic compounds caused by flare-ups when you grill over direct heat. Whether or not these marinades are good for you, they will make your palate feel very happy and healthy!

HERBED wet RUB

Makes about 2 cups | 500 mL

This is a cross between a marinade and a paste. It is superb on any meat. Make it a bit thinner with the addition of more olive oil and you can toss vegetables in it to roast on the grill. It's even great tossed with some fresh cooked pasta!

2 loosely packed cups | 500 mL fresh chopped herbs (use equal parts of fresh Italian parsley, mint, basil, cilantro, baby dill, sage, or any combination that goes with what you want to grill)

6 cloves garlic, peeled

1 shallot, peeled and coarsely chopped

1 Tbsp. | 15 mL chopped chives

1 tsp. | 5 mL Dijon mustard

1 tsp. | 5 mL kosher salt

up to 1 cup | 250 mL oil (extra virgin if you're going with a Mediterranean theme, or a more neutral-flavored oil, like canola, if you're cooking Asian or Southwestern)

Combine the herbs, garlic, shallot, chives, mustard and salt in a food processor and whiz until everything is finely chopped. Keep the processor running and slowly add the oil until the mixture looks like a thin paste (or a very thick marinade.) Coat whatever you're grilling with the mixture and let sit in the fridge for 1/2 to 1 hour for veggies and seafood and anywhere from 2 hours to overnight for meat. This rub does not keep well, so make it right when you need it.

ASIAN poultry BRINE

Makes enough for 2 cut up chickens or a dozen thighs

The high salt content makes this more of a brine than a marinade, and my barbecue team has used it very successfully in competition. It gives the poultry a nice saltiness and a rich, complex Asian flavor. I marinate duck overnight in this; for milder-tasting chicken, a couple of hours is all you need. Pat excess moisture from the meat after you've taken it out of the marinade and then use a barbecue rub doctored with Asian flavors, like powdered ginger and five-spice powder. Barbecue or grill as you like, and finish with your favorite barbecue sauce.

1½ cups | 375 mL water

1 cup | 250 mL soy sauce

1/2 cup | 125 mL sherry or vermouth

1/2 cup | 125 mL apple or pineapple juice

1/4 cup | 50 mL brown sugar

1/4 cup | 50 mL coarse salt

2 cloves garlic, pressed or crushed

1 shallot, minced

1 medium onion, thinly sliced

2 Tbsp. | 25 mL grated fresh ginger

1 tsp. | 5 mL sesame oil

pinch ground cloves

pinch five-spice powder

Combine all ingredients well, stirring thoroughly to dissolve the salt and sugar.

marinade FOR PORK

Makes enough marinade for up to 2 lbs. | 1 kg of pork chops or whole tenderloins

Pork tastes great no matter how you prepare it, but this sweet, aromatic marinade nicely offsets its richness and gives it an exotic edge.

1/4 cup | 50 mL soy sauce

2 Tbsp. | 25 mL dry sherry

2 Tbsp. | 25 mL honey

2 Tbsp. | 25 mL brown sugar

1 tsp. | 5 mL salt

1/2 tsp. | 2 mL crushed anise seed

1/2 tsp. | 2 mL ground cinnamon

1/8 tsp. | 1/2 mL ground cloves

1 Tbsp. | 15 mL grated fresh ginger

Combine all ingredients in a saucepan and heat gently until the sugar is dissolved. Cool before marinating meat for at least an hour, or overnight in the fridge if you want a stronger flavor.

SAUCES

Texas red sauce. Eastern North Carolina mustard sauce. North Alabama white sauce. Louisiana Creole–style sauce. The list of regional American barbecue sauces goes on and on, and rivalries between states, regions and restaurants continue unabated. And never mind which sauce to use. There's a big debate about whether real barbecue should have any sauce at all, and some of the oldest barbecue restaurants in America don't even offer sauce to customers. On the other hand, most definitions of barbecue include a reference to sauce, and just about every barbecue cook has his or her own unique take on it. In my opinion, sauce is one of the things that defines barbecue. Its sweetness and acidity contrast with, and therefore help to intensify, the savory flavor of the meat. Think of these recipes as starting points for you to devise your own signature sauce.

ron's rich, DEEPLY SATISFYING dipping SAUCE

(WITH ACKNOWLEDGMENTS TO THE BARON OF BARBECUE, PAUL KIRK)

Makes about 6 cups | 1.5 L

BARBECUE ➣ SECRET ≈

Use sauce sparingly when grilling or barbecuing meat. In competition we use it only as a finishing glaze. If you baste meat with a sugary sauce more than an hour before you take it out of the smoker or more than a few minutes before removing it from the grill, it will turn black when the sugar caramelizes from the heat. Also use sauce sparingly when you serve, offering it to guests on the side. Too much sauce and you lose the barbecue flavor you've worked so hard to achieve!

Any student of barbecue has to bow in the direction of Kansas City once in a while, and Paul Kirk is one of the world's greatest barbecue cooks and also perhaps its best-known ambassador. Paul has taught thousands of cooks the essentials of barbecue, and this rich, sweet, tangy sauce is based on his Kansas City classic.

2 Tbsp. | 25 mL powdered ancho, poblano or New Mexico chiles

1 Tbsp. | 15 mL ground black pepper

1 Tbsp. | 15 mL dry mustard

1 tsp. | 5 mL ground coriander

1 tsp. | 5 mL ground allspice

1/4 tsp. | 1 mL ground cloves

1/2 tsp. | 2 mL grated nutmeg

up to 1 tsp. | 5 mL cayenne, according to your taste

1/4 cup | 50 mL neutral-flavored oil, such as canola

1 onion, finely chopped

6 cloves garlic, finely chopped

1 shallot, minced

1/2 cup | 125 mL tightly packed dark brown sugar

1 cup | 250 mL white vinegar

1/2 cup | 125 mL clover honey

1/4 cup | 50 mL Worcestershire sauce or soy sauce
or a combination

1 tsp. | 5 mL liquid smoke or hickory smoked salt (optional)

1 32-oz. | 1-L keg of ketchup

Mix all the spices together and set aside. Heat the oil in a big pot over medium heat and gently sauté the onion, garlic and shallot until tender. Add the spices and mix thoroughly, cooking for 2 or 3 minutes to bring out their flavors. Add the remaining ingredients and simmer the mixture for 30 minutes, stirring often (be careful, it spatters). Don't cook it too long or it will start to caramelize and you'll have spicy fudge. If you want a very smooth sauce, blend with a hand blender or food processor. Preserve as you would a jam or jelly in mason jars. Use as a glaze or a dip for barbecued meats, or as a flavoring sauce in fajitas.

VINCE STATEN'S hacking sauce

Makes about 2 cups | 500 mL

My friend Kathy found this in a food magazine, and apparently it's the best way to cure a cold. Make it a week or so in advance and let the flavors become well acquainted. Drizzle this over your pulled pork sandwich before applying coleslaw.

1/3 cup | 75 mL apple cider vinegar

1 tsp. | 5 mL salt

1 tsp. | 5 mL celery seed

1 tsp. | 5 mL ancho chile powder

1/2 tsp. | 2 mL cinnamon

1/2 tsp. | 2 mL cayenne

1/2 tsp. | 2 mL brown sugar

1/2 cup | 125 mL ketchup

1/8 tsp. | 1/2 mL nutmeg

1 cup | 250 mL water

1 Tbsp. | 15 mL your favorite cough syrup

Combine the ingredients in a saucepan and bring to a boil. Cool and refrigerate. It stores indefinitely.

complicated BUT DELICIOUS TERIYAKI sauce

Makes about 8 cups | 2 L

This homemade teriyaki sauce, which I have slightly adapted from a recipe by famed Vancouver chef Trevor Hooper, has dimensions of flavor that make the extra work more than worthwhile. It stores for several months in the fridge.

1¹/₂ cups | 375 mL sake

1¹/₂ cups | 375 mL mirin

2 cups | 500 mL brown sugar

4 cups | 1 L Japanese soy sauce

1/2 cup | 125 mL tamari soy sauce

1 small onion, chopped

1 shallot, chopped

4 cloves garlic, chopped

1 2-inch | 5-cm piece fresh ginger, chopped

1 orange, chopped, skin on

1 small pear, chopped

1 small leek, split, washed thoroughly and chopped

Combine all ingredients in a medium saucepan and bring to a low boil. Cook until reduced by about 20 percent. Cool, strain into a large jar or bottle, and refrigerate.

PIGPEN'S secret SAUCE

Makes about 8 cups | 2 L

My friend and barbecue teammate Kathy Richardier discovered this sauce in a mystery novel set against the backdrop of competitive barbecue. This recipe is on the last page, and Kathy says history will treat the sauce recipe better than the book!

2 cups | 500 mL apple cider (Kathy uses Symond's Scrumpy Jack)

1/2 cup | 125 mL balsamic vinegar

1¼ cups | 300 mL ketchup

1/2 cup | 125 mL honey mustard

1/2 cup | 125 mL yellow mustard

1/2 cup | 125 mL coarse-grained mustard

1/2 cup | 125 mL honey

1/2 cup | 125 mL molasses

1/2 cup | 125 mL cane syrup
(try the English kind called Lyle's Golden Syrup)

1 12-oz. | 355-mL bottle dark beer
(Kathy uses Henry Weinhard's dark beer)

1/2 cup | 125 mL strong black coffee

1/8 cup | 25 mL Worcestershire sauce

1/8 cup | 25 mL soy sauce

1/8 cup | 25 mL Louisiana hot sauce

1 tsp. | 5 mL ground pepper

1 tsp. | 5 mL celery salt

**1 habañero chile, seeds removed and diced
(or throw in a huge shot of Sriracha or other Asian hot chili sauce)**

pinch kosher salt

pinch ground coriander

Combine all ingredients and simmer half an hour or so. This is a fairly thin sauce and makes a good marinade for chicken. It's also good brushed on hamburgers, lamburgers, turkeyburgers... or just eat it out of the jar with a spoon. Keeps for a few months in the fridge.

north carolina–style VINEGAR sauce

Makes a little over 1 cup | 250 mL

This is old-school barbecue sauce at its finest. Drizzle some of this into pulled pork just before serving to give it some classic heat and tang, or use it to baste pork butt.

1 cup | 250 mL white vinegar

1 cup | 250 mL cider vinegar

2 Tbsp. | 15 mL brown sugar

1 Tbsp. | 15 mL crushed dried chiles

1 tsp. | 5 mL Louisiana–style hot pepper sauce

salt and pepper to taste

Combine all ingredients and stir until the sugar is dissolved. Stores indefinitely in the fridge.

classic mustard-BASED BARBECUE sauce

Makes about 2 cups | 500 mL

Who knows why most barbecue sauces are sweet and tomato-based? This tangy, mustardy style sauce is very much alive in the Carolinas and Georgia, but almost unheard of most other places. It's delicious, of course, with pork.

1 medium onion, finely minced

4 cloves garlic, finely minced

2 Tbsp. | 25 mL vegetable oil

1 cup | 250 mL cider vinegar

2/3 cup prepared mustard

1/3 cup | 75 mL brown sugar

1 Tbsp. | 15 mL ancho chile powder

1 Tbsp. | 15 mL paprika

1 tsp. | 5 mL finely ground black pepper

1/4 tsp. | 1 mL cayenne

2 Tbsp. | 25 mL butter or margarine

dash of soy sauce or Worcestershire sauce

Over low to medium heat, gently sauté the onion and garlic in the vegetable oil until soft but not browned. Add the vinegar, mustard, brown sugar, chile powder, paprika, pepper and cayenne. Bring to a boil and simmer for 10 minutes. Stir in the butter or margarine and soy or Worcestershire sauce and remove from the heat. If you prefer a smoother sauce to one with little chunks of onion and garlic, purée with a hand blender before serving. This sauce is good warm, but it stores indefinitely in the fridge.

asian BARBECUE sauce

A Toast to Spices and Nuts!

In India, the first step in almost every home-cooked dish is to toast some spices in a hot pan. The heat refreshes the spices, bringing to life the natural oils that carry their flavor. This technique works especially well with robust whole spices like cumin, coriander and fennel seeds. All you have to do is preheat a dry frying pan on a medium setting and toss in a handful of seeds. Shake the pan constantly, watching carefully. After about a minute, when they start to brown a little and give off a strong aroma, empty the pan into a cool bowl or plate to stop the toasting before they burn. In a few minutes the seeds are ready to go into a spice mill, mortar or coffee grinder. The difference between raw and toasted spices is like night and day.

This technique also works fabulously with pecans or other nuts, sesame seeds, pumpkin seeds and pine nuts. Toast up a handful of nuts and sprinkle some on a salad for sharp, crunchy bursts of nutty flavor!

The cumin seeds in this sauce give it a Southwestern twist and an interesting texture. Leave them out if you want a slightly sweeter sauce. This is great as a marinade and a basting sauce for ribs and steaks but is also good with chicken and firm-fleshed fish. Be careful—its strong flavors can overwhelm what you're cooking. Marinate for a maximum of 4 hours for meat and 1 hour for chicken and fish.

1 12-ounce | 355-mL bottle hoisin sauce

1/2 cup | 125 mL light soy sauce

2 Tbsp. | 25 mL sherry vinegar

juice of 1 orange

1/2 cup | 125 mL plum sauce

1/2 Tbsp. | 7 mL five-spice powder

2 Tbsp. | 25 mL toasted sesame oil

2 Tbsp. | 25 mL oyster sauce

6 cloves garlic, finely minced

2 shallots, finely minced

2 Tbsp. | 25 mL finely minced fresh ginger

2 Tbsp. | 25 mL honey

1 Tbsp. | 15 mL finely chopped chives or green onion

1 tsp. | 5 mL whole toasted cumin seeds

Mix all the ingredients together in a nonreactive bowl. Use soon after making; it won't keep more than a few days in the fridge.

All the Fixin's: Starters and Sides

Chapter IV

STARTERS

When you're having people over to enjoy some of your backyard cookery, you need to give them something to eat before dinner because otherwise they'll get drunk, start to argue and someone will pass out on your carpet. At the same time, you don't want to stuff them with appetizers because they will want to have big helpings of whatever succulent fare you've got going on your grill or in your smoker. Whatever you make, keep the portions small and make them easy to grab and eat while holding a drink.

a QUESADILLA library

Easy to make and quick to cook, quesadillas are the perfect summer party food. Think of the soft flour tortilla as a palette upon which you can paint beautiful tastescapes for your guests. Or something like that. Preparing a quesadilla is as easy as one, two, three, four, five.

1. **Place a large flour tortilla on a cutting board or cookie sheet and cover it with a 1/4-inch | 5-mm layer of shredded cheese. (What you want is a gooey but bland cheese like mozzarella or Jack for the right texture, plus, if you want to get fancy, a more robust-tasting cheese like Asiago, Gouda or blue cheese for extra flavor.)**

2. **Layer on the toppings, taking care to distribute them evenly.**

3. **Sprinkle the toppings with salt, pepper and a little hot sauce to taste. (If you've used a salty cheese like blue, go easy.)**

4. **Coat with another thin layer of shredded cheese.**

5. **Top with another flour tortilla.**

To cook, preheat your charcoal or gas grill to a medium-high heat. Place the quesadilla directly on the grill and cook for 2 or 3 minutes, until the cheese starts to melt and the tortilla is toasted and slightly charred. Flip with a big spatula and cook the other side for another 2 or 3 minutes. Take it off the grill, place it on a cutting board and let it rest for a minute or two. Cut it into pizza-like slices with a big sharp knife.

Accompany with fresh salsa, guacamole and sour cream for dipping. Quesadillas can also easily be made on a stovetop or on the propane burner on the side of your grill in a large, lightly oiled skillet over medium-high heat. You can prepare the quesadillas in advance and keep them covered and refrigerated for an hour or two before grilling (if you try to keep them overnight the tortillas will get soggy).

Variations

Classic
Equal parts shredded Asiago and Jack cheese, with pickled jalapeño slices, a bit of tomato salsa and some chopped cilantro, salt and pepper. Sour cream and guacamole are perfect accompaniments.

Hiker's Dream (from Calgary foodie Gail Norton)
Equal parts shredded Jack and smoked Gouda, thinly sliced Granny Smith apple, fresh chopped rosemary, salt and pepper. Unusual and delicious!

Funky
Shredded Jack cheese, chunks of chèvre (creamy goat cheese), slices of roasted red pepper, lightly toasted pine nuts, salt and pepper. Serve with jalapeño jelly.

Heavenly
Shredded Jack cheese, chopped cilantro and a few spoonfuls of leftover chili or chorizo. Dip in sour cream or fresh salsa.

Wolfgangpuckadilla
Shredded Jack cheese with daubs of cream cheese, slices of lox, a few capers, some thinly sliced red onion, salt and pepper. Serve with sour cream and...caviar?

Blue Cheese Dream
Shredded Jack, crumbled strong blue cheese like Roquefort or Gorgonzola, ripe pear slices.

Calicado
Shredded Jack with chopped pitted canned black olives, avocado slices, chopped cilantro, chopped fresh red bell pepper, salt, pepper and a squeeze of fresh lime.

Tropical
Mozzarella and Brie, thinly sliced ripe mango or papaya, chopped cilantro, thinly sliced onion and chopped fresh jalapeño. Serve with sour cream as a dip.

Simple but Great
Just plain shredded Jack or Cheddar cheese with pickled jalapeños.

≻ NOTE ≺

Flavored cheeses like jalapeño Jack, peppered goat cheese or spiced Gouda are excellent in quesadillas.

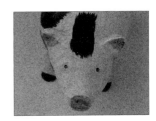

easiest ever APPETIZER

Serves 2 to 6 depending on size of eaters and their appetites

Delish and quick, perfect for hungry teens. Serve this dip with corn or potato chips.

**1 can (14 oz. | 398 mL) of your favorite tinned chili,
the spicier the better**

1 package softened cream cheese

Mix together and heat in a covered dish in your microwave until hot.

CHIPOTLE and roasted GARLIC aïoli

Makes about 1½ cups | 375 mL

I've added a little cumin to this Southwestern take on aïoli from friend and caterer Margie Gibb. This is outrageously good with pretty much anything. Try it as a dip with grilled vegetables or cut-up smoked sausages, or use it as a spread in burgers and other sandwiches.

1½ cups | 375 mL good-quality store-bought mayonnaise or homemade aïoli (see below)

1 whole head roasted garlic, squeezed out of its skin

1 tsp. | 5 mL finely ground cumin (preferably made from toasted cumin seeds)

1 Tbsp. | 15 mL chopped chipotles in adobo sauce (add more of the chipotles if you like it hot)

Combine the ingredients in a food processor. Refrigerate for at least a few hours before you are going to use it, and preferably overnight, to give time for the flavors to marry. If made with purchased mayo, it will last a couple of months in the fridge. Use it within a few days if you're using homemade aïoli with fresh raw eggs.

aïoli

2 large egg yolks

2 Tbsp. | 25 mL lemon juice

1¼ cups | 300 mL extra virgin olive oil

kosher salt and freshly ground black pepper to taste

In the bowl of a food processor, combine the egg yolks and lemon juice; process for 5 seconds. With the machine running, drizzle the olive oil through the feed tube in a slow steady stream, processing until combined. Season with salt and pepper. It will keep refrigerated for up to 3 days.

Roasted Garlic

Roasting turns pungent garlic into a golden brown, soft, sweet, spreadable delight that's great in mashed potatoes and dips, or spread on toasted French bread.

Preheat the oven to 350°F/175°C. With a sharp knife, slice off the top of a garlic bulb, just enough to expose the tops of each of the cloves. Set on a piece of foil, drizzle with a little olive oil, season with salt and pepper and wrap the bulb tightly in foil. Place in the oven, cut side up, and roast for about an hour, or until the garlic is soft and lightly browned. Once it is cool enough to handle, you can squeeze the head and the roasted garlic comes out like toothpaste.

BARBECUE ⇝ SECRET ≈

Roast garlic in your smoker (for 3 hours) or over medium in-direct heat in a covered charcoal grill (for 1 hour) to add an extra layer of smokey flavor to the garlic. Just wrap the garlic fairly loosely in foil to allow the smoke to get in. Excellent with cherry wood as the flavoring agent. An added benefit: you don't stink up your house.

GRILLED vegetable platter

Serves 10 to 20, depending on what else you've got going

There's almost nothing as boring as a bunch of raw celery, carrots, radishes and broccoli florets on a plate with a bowl of seasoned yoghurt in the middle. Add some excitement to veggies by grilling them and serving with a couple of interesting dips. The key here is to not overdo the vegetables. Each vegetable cooks a little differently; zucchini and asparagus cook the fastest and the cauliflower will take the longest to grill. This recipe is pretty elaborate and is designed for when you're entertaining. For everyday cooking, just grill one or two kinds of veggies and they're ready in minutes. For a party, serve as an appetizer along with quesadillas and perhaps some kebabs. They are delicious on their own, but go even better with a nice dip, like Chipotle and Roasted Garlic Aïoli (page 73) or Sesame Mayonnaise (page 105). Grilled veggies are also great tossed into a green salad or served as a side with grilled meat or fish. To add more flavor, before grilling toss with some dried or fresh chopped herbs like rosemary, oregano or basil.

20 nugget potatoes, skins on

20 cauliflower florets (about 1 head of cauliflower)

4 sweet potatoes, peeled and cut into rounds 1/2 inch | 1 cm thick

2 red bell peppers cut lengthwise into 2-inch | 5-cm strips

2 yellow bell peppers cut lengthwise into 2-inch | 5-cm strips

2 green bell peppers cut lengthwise into 2-inch | 5-cm strips

2 bunches fresh asparagus spears, tough ends snapped off

4 zucchini, cut lengthwise into 1/2-inch | 1-cm slabs

20 whole ripe cherry tomatoes

1 cup | 250 mL extra virgin olive oil

kosher salt and freshly ground black pepper to taste

3 fresh lemons, cut into wedges

In a large pot of cold water over high heat, bring the potatoes to a boil. Turn down the heat and simmer for 10 minutes, adding the cauliflower florets when you have 5 minutes to go. Remove from the pot and cool the potatoes and cauliflower in a bowl of cold water. Drain again and set aside.

Preheat your charcoal or gas grill for medium direct heat.

Put all the vegetables in a large bowl, in batches if necessary, and toss with the extra virgin olive oil, kosher salt and freshly ground pepper and herbs if desired. Grill the vegetables over high direct heat, starting with the sweet potatoes, potatoes and cauliflower, turning often. Grill the tenderest vegetables last, taking care not to overcook the asparagus, zucchini and cherry tomatoes (which really only need to be heated through).

Arrange all the grilled vegetables on a big platter, drizzle with a little more oil and serve immediately. Garnish with lemon wedges. You can also make this an hour or two ahead of time and serve at room temperature.

NOTE

You can grill almost any vegetable, in any quantity, simply by tossing the veggies in olive oil, sprinkling them with salt and putting them on a hot grill. The more robust the vegetable, the longer the cooking time. The more you grill, the better you'll get!

sesame MAYONNAISE

Makes about 1 cup | 250 mL

This wonderful, Asian-influenced mayonnaise can be tweaked to your heart's content and your tongue's preference. It's perfect with cold asparagus but would also complement almost anything on a platter of blanched or grilled vegetables, as well as hard-boiled eggs, cold salmon or shrimp, grilled or blanched veggies, or sliced or chunked avocado with a squeeze of lime juice. Sprinkle some toasted sesame seeds on top for added texture.

1 cup | 250 mL real mayonnaise

1 tsp. | 5 mL toasted sesame oil

1/2 tsp. | 2 mL soy sauce (or to taste)

1 tsp. | 5 mL Chinese chili sauce or
spicy Szechuan chili oil (or to taste)

grated and finely chopped fresh lemon, lime or orange rind

a squeeze of lemon, lime or orange juice

1 to 2 Tbsp. | 15 to 25 mL toasted sesame seeds (to taste)

Whisk everything but the sesame seeds together and taste, adding more of the flavors you like best. Chill so they have time to marry. Garnish with toasted sesame seeds.

MARK'S otherworldly TACO filling

Makes about 4 servings

We've all had tacos made with ground beef and commercial "taco seasoning"—a cheap, sorry imitation of this wonderful dish, which is a staple food in Latin America. This rich, luxurious "chorizo" (a kind of loose version of what we normally think of as Spanish sausage) comes from famous Southwestern chef Mark Miller's ground-breaking *Coyote Café* cookbook. It's a great filling for quesadillas, tacos or burritos. You can also mix it with scrambled eggs, spice up a soup with it or just eat it right out of the pot. When I make it I usually double or triple the recipe and freeze some for future use.

1 lb. | 500 g fresh ground pork

1/2 lb. | 250 g fresh lean ground beef

2 small cloves garlic, finely minced

4 Tbsp. | 60 mL ancho or New Mexico chili powder

1/2 tsp. | 2 mL cayenne

1/8 tsp. | 1/2 mL ground cloves

1/2 tsp. | 2 mL freshly ground black pepper

2 tsp. | 10 mL ground cinnamon

1 tsp. | 5 mL ground cumin

1 tsp. | 5 mL kosher salt

3 cups | 750 mL water

In a heavy skillet or big pot, fry the pork and beef over medium heat. Break up with a wooden spoon and do not allow to brown. Add the garlic, spices, salt and 1 cup / 250 mL of the water. Cook slowly over low heat for at least an hour to allow the flavors to marry. Add extra water as needed, though the finished mixture should not be wet; all the excess water should have evaporated and the chorizo should be cooking in its own fat (which you shouldn't drain off because it is so full of flavor!). Adjust final seasonings by adding salt and pepper to taste.

BACON-wrapped oysters

Serves 4 to 6 as an appetizer

This old-fashioned and simple way to grill oysters makes a great party appetizer.

**1-pint | 500-mL container large fresh shucked oysters
(about a dozen oysters)**

1/4 lb. | 125 g thinly sliced bacon, each slice cut in half

kosher salt and freshly ground pepper to taste

Louisiana–style hot sauce

In a heavy skillet fry the bacon over medium heat until it is cooked but not quite crispy. Place the cooked bacon strips on a paper towel and set aside. Prepare your grill for direct high heat. Drain the oysters and pat dry with a paper towel. Wrap half a slice of cooked bacon around each oyster, skewering it with a wooden toothpick. Place the oysters on the cooking grate and grill for 2 or 3 minutes per side or until the bacon crisps and the oysters are cooked through and just starting to char. Remove from the heat, place on a platter, season with salt and pepper and pass them around with a bottle of hot sauce.

smoked**TOMATO**guacamole

Makes about 2 cups | 500 mL

Everybody has their favorite recipe for guacamole but the flavor of the freshly smoked ripe tomatoes in this one really jolts your tastebuds! If you're in a hurry, it also tastes great without smoking the tomatoes. Serve this with corn tortilla chips. It's also very nice on grilled fish or chicken.

2 ripe tomatoes

2 large, ripe but still firm avocados

juice of two limes or one lemon

1 clove garlic, minced

2 Tbsp. | 25 mL chopped cilantro

3 tinned green chiles, rinsed, seeded and chopped

2 or 3 pickled jalapeño or serrano chiles, minced (optional)

kosher salt

Prepare your smoker for barbecuing, bringing the temperature up to 200–220°F/95–100°C. (Obviously it's easier if you're barbecuing something else and the smoker is already chugging away.) Place the tomatoes in the smoker and cook for 30 minutes, using a hardwood like hickory or mesquite as a flavoring agent. The idea is to infuse the tomatoes with smoke without overcooking them—when ready, they should be a red-gold color and their skins should be a bit loose, but the flesh should still be firm.

Coarsely chop the tomatoes and flesh of the avocados, combine in a bowl and blend in lime or lemon juice, garlic, chopped cilantro, green chiles, smoked tomato, and hot chiles. Season to taste with salt.

SMOKE IT WHILE YOU'VE GOT IT

Your smoker or barbecue pit takes awhile to get going, and it chugs away after you've finished cooking. It's a shame to waste all those good vapors. Once your smoker is going, take advantage of the situation by smoking other foods to eat another time. Cheap breakfast sausages turn to gold, both figuratively and literally, with a couple hours in the smoker. Smoked chicken refrigerates and freezes well and you can fit 4 to 6 whole birds in a small water smoker. You can smoke almost anything. Try some of these ideas.

- Hard-boil some eggs until they are just done, peel them and put them in your smoker for half an hour to an hour, or until the eggs take on a light golden color. Adds a certain what-the-heck-is-that-delicious-taste to your deviled eggs or egg salad.

- Smoke fresh, ripe tomatoes for about half an hour—just until they are infused with smoke but the flesh is still firm. Use them wherever you'd use fresh tomatoes and give your salsa, guacamole, pasta sauce or salad a smokey kick.

- Peel and cut some onions in half, or in ½-inch / 1-cm rounds, and toss them into the smoker for an hour. They make delicious onion soup, and they freeze well. Also try smoking garlic cloves in the skin, or roasting whole heads.

- Put a cup or two of kosher or Malden salt in a cake pan and put it in the smoker. Smoked salt allows you to give a rich smokey flavor to anything without having to fire up the cooker.

- Nuts—especially almonds and pecans—take to smoking extremely well. Toss them with a little neutral-flavored oil and some of your barbecue rub, curry powder, Louisiana–style hot sauce or other seasonings and place them in a cake pan or on a greased sheet of foil big enough to hold them in one layer. Smoke for about an hour. They're great fresh out of the cooker but you can store them for a few days in a covered container.

- Duck is one of the very best smoked meats and it freezes well. Barbecue half ducks using the usual mustard-and-rub technique, but doctor your Classic Barbecue Rub with a Tbsp. / 15 mL each of powdered ginger, mustard powder and five-spice powder.

Classic North Carolina Barbecued Pulled Pork Sandwich
page 126

Beef Burger with Herbed Butter Core and Caramelized Onions
page 118

Cowboy Steak with Supercharged Corn on the Cob
pages 143 and 90

Rack of Lamb with Balsamic Reduction
page 158

enoteca SMOKED DUCK salad

Serves 8 as an appetizer or 4 as a main course for lunch

My wife, Kate, found this recipe many years ago in a 1990s collection of recipes from American bistros. Seattle's Enoteca does not exist any more, but as long as I barbecue, I will have this recipe in my repertoire. I like to keep a few smoked duck halves in the freezer in case we have dinner guests we want to blow away. The original recipe calls for fresh papaya, which is excellent, but I like slightly tangier mango as the fruit component.

For the dressing

1/2 cup | 125 mL soy sauce

2/3 cup | 150 mL red wine vinegar

1/2 cup | 125 mL sugar

4 Tbsp. | 60 mL vegetable oil

4 Tbsp. | 60 mL rice wine vinegar

4 Tbsp. | 60 mL raspberry vinegar

juice of 1 lime

For the salad

1 pound smoked duck or smoked chicken
(see chart on page 29 for technique)

2 whole fresh mangoes

2 bags fresh baby spinach,
washed and dried well

1/2 small purple onion, diced

freshly ground pepper

juice of 1 lime

1 cup | 250 mL toasted and coarsely
chopped walnuts or pecans

1 lime, quartered, for garnish

To prepare the dressing, bring the soy sauce, vinegar, sugar and oil to a boil. Cook until the sugar is dissolved. Add the remaining ingredients and let cool. This makes enough dressing for 4 salads, but it keeps for at least a few weeks in the refrigerator.

Cut the smoked duck into bite-sized pieces. (If you are using duck that is frozen, thaw it first, heat it up in a 350°F/180°C oven, then let it rest until cool enough to handle.) Peel the mangoes and slice the flesh off the pits; reserve a few slices for garnish. Place the spinach, duck, mango and onion in a salad bowl. Grind the pepper over the mixture and squeeze the lime juice over it. Add the nuts and just enough dressing to coat and toss. (Too much dressing drowns out the other salad fixings.) Garnish the salad with the lime quarters and the reserved mango slices.

smoked **SHRIMP**

Makes an appetizer for 4 to 6

Fellow Butt Shredder Vince Gogolek has perfected this recipe, which uses a brine to firm the flesh of the shrimp and add a nice salty flavor. Eat them straight off the smoker as a snack. They are also a superb addition to either Alfredo or marinara sauce. Add them at the end of cooking the sauce, just long enough to heat them through and serve with your favorite pasta. You will have way more brine than you need for this much shrimp, so buy a few fresh trout and brine and smoke them, using the same method, while you're at it!

4 qts. | 4 L water

2 cups | 500 mL salt (use kosher or pickling salt, not iodized)

1/4 lb. | 125 g brown sugar

1/3 cup | 75 mL lemon juice

1 Tbsp. | 15 mL minced garlic or 1 tsp. | 5 mL garlic salt

1 Tbsp. | 15 mL minced onion or 1 tsp. | 5 mL onion salt

1 tsp. | 5 mL Louisiana–style hot sauce (optional)

1 lb. | 500 g peeled, deveined shrimp

Prepare your smoker for barbecuing, bringing the temperature up to 200–220°F / 95–100°C.

Combine all the ingredients except for the shrimp. You will have way more brine than you need for this much shrimp, so buy a few fresh trout and brine and smoke them, using the same method, while you're at it! Soak the shrimp in enough brine to cover for about 30 minutes. If they stay in the brine too long, they will take on an unpleasant, very salty taste, and will have to be rinsed extensively to make them palatable. Make sure to remove the shrimp from the brine and let them sit for about 10 minutes on a drying rack before putting them in the smoker.

Smoke them for about 30 minutes. Because of the short cooking time, you can prepare several batches of shrimp over a couple of hours. When they are pink they are done, and like any seafood you don't want to overcook them. Serve just as they are, stabbed with toothpicks on a serving tray, with perhaps some doctored mayo as a dip.

the deviled EGGS went down to GEORGIA

Makes 2 dozen devilled eggs

You don't see much of this old-fashioned appetizer, but smoking the eggs makes it modern again.

12 eggs

1/2 cup | 50 mL Chipotle and Roasted Garlic Aioli (page 73)

1 Tbsp. | 15 mL Dijon mustard

2 Tbsp. | 25 mL finely chopped cilantro

1 lemon

1 tsp. | 5 mL paprika

sprigs cilantro, for garnish

Choose eggs that are at least a few days old (fresh eggs are harder to peel). Put them in a pot of lukewarm water with a bit of vinegar added. Bring to a boil and remove from the heat the moment the water begins to boil. Leave the eggs in the water for 15 minutes, then cool under cold running water and peel. Prepare your smoker for barbecuing, bringing the temperature up to 200–220°F/95–100°C. Place the eggs on the cooking grate and smoke for about half an hour using hickory, maple or oak as the flavoring agent. Sprinkle lightly with dry rub if you want a little more flavor. The eggs will turn an amber color. Let them cool. Slice them in half lengthwise and remove the yolks, setting the whites aside. In a nonreactive bowl, mash the yolks with a fork and add the aïoli, mustard and cilantro, along with the juice of half the lemon. Mix thoroughly and spoon or pipe the mixture back into the egg whites. Sprinkle with paprika and garnish with cilantro sprigs and lemon slices.

TOFU kebabs

Makes 6 to 8 kebabs

Some of my best friends are vegetarians. I am proud to have converted at least one or two, but those who decide to stay on the other side have to eat, too. Tofu is great because it takes on other flavors so easily. This recipe comes from my activist friend Stuart Parker. Serve these kebabs as an alternate main course or appetizer for non-meat-eaters.

1/3 cup | 75 mL Japanese or Korean soy sauce

1 cup | 500 mL Chinese black vinegar

2/3 cup | 150 mL water

6 Tbsp. | 90 mL grated fresh ginger

Thai sambal sauce (optional) to taste

1 lb. | 500 g firm tofu

1 red bell pepper, cut into bite-size chunks

1 yellow bell pepper, cut into bite-size chunks

1 green bell pepper, cut into bite-size chunks

1 medium white onion, cut into bite-size chunks

12 to 16 small white button mushrooms

1/4 cup | 50 mL peanut oil

kosher salt and freshly ground black pepper to taste

Combine the soy sauce, vinegar, water, ginger and sambal sauce, if desired, in a nonreactive bowl. Cut the tofu into 3/4-inch/2-cm cubes and marinate for a minimum of 8 hours, but ideally overnight. To determine if the tofu is sufficiently marinated, cut it to see if the color of the marinade has permeated through the entire cube. Presoak bamboo skewers.

Prepare your grill for medium direct heat. Cut the bell peppers and onion into bite-sized chunks. Thread the tofu onto the skewers, alternating with mushrooms, bell pepper and onion. For crispier kebabs, brush the tofu and vegetables with peanut oil before placing on the grill. Grill for 6 to 8 minutes, turning 2 or 3 times, until the tofu is cooked through and vegetables are nicely charred. Season with salt and pepper and serve.

smoked ONION soup

Serves 6

Take advantage when your smoker is chugging away to smoke some onions for later use. The flavor of this soup, which was perfected by my friend Gail Norton, depends on the length of time the onions are smoked and the type of wood used (hickory for a darker, richer flavor, fruitwood for a lighter, sweeter taste). The cream tends to smooth the smoke flavor, but it can be omitted.

4 large onions

3 Tbsp. | 45 mL butter

1/4 cup | 50 mL olive oil

2 cloves garlic, finely minced

1 tsp. | 5 mL kosher salt

2 tsp. | 10 mL sugar

freshly ground black pepper to taste

1 cup | 250 mL red wine

1/4 cup | 50 mL all-purpose flour

6 cups | 1.5 L warm beef broth

1 cup | 250 mL whipping cream

Prepare your smoker for barbecuing, bringing the temperature up to 200–220°F/95–100°C. Peel and slice the onions and cut into 1/4 to 1/2-inch/5 to 10-mm rounds. Smoke, using hickory or fruitwood as a flavoring agent, for about an hour or until the onions have taken on a golden color. Remove from the smoker and set aside. (The onions can be smoked and frozen for several months.)

Melt the butter in a large pot and add the olive oil. When the oil is hot, add the onions and cook over medium-high heat, stirring frequently. Brown them well (this might take up to half an hour), but be careful not to burn them. Once the onions are well caramelized, add the garlic, turn down the heat and cook for about 5 minutes longer. Add the salt, sugar and pepper.

Add the red wine and reduce to a jam-like consistency. Add the flour, stir to incorporate well, and begin adding the warmed beef broth, a cup at a time, stirring constantly. Allow the soup to simmer for about 30 minutes or until you can no longer taste the flour. Add the cream and heat thoroughly without boiling.

SIDES

This is a barbecue cookbook, so I'm not going to get fancy here. When you are entertaining using your grill or barbecue, the meat is the center of attention and what you want are things that complement it, like beans, cornbread, corn on the cob and coleslaw. Save your fancy hors d'oeuvres for indoor meals. Here are several superb variations on the classic accompaniments.

RED beans

Serves about 10

Sometimes the simplest things are the best. This is how my Texan friend Amy Walker's mom makes beans. It's a simple recipe but requires some tending, so it's best made on an afternoon when you have other tasks in the kitchen or the backyard. This is definitely worth the effort!

3 cups | 750 mL dried pinto beans

1/2-lb. | 250-g chunk salt pork, cut in 2 pieces

In a large nonreactive bowl, soak the beans in water overnight, or at least 5 hours. Drain and rinse the beans, discarding the old water. Place the beans in a large pot, add water to cover and bring to a boil. Turn the heat down to low and simmer the beans for about 2 hours or until tender. Stir occasionally to keep them from sticking to the bottom of the pot, and add boiling water as necessary as the beans soak up the water. (Tip: keep a kettle of warm water on the stove, so that when you need to add water the beans will keep boiling.) During the second hour, test for tenderness by squashing some of the beans against the side of the pot with your stirring spoon. Keep the squashed ones in the pot to help make good soupy beans. Also taste them once in a while to see if they are soft. During the second hour add the salt pork. (Be sure not to add it too soon, or the beans will be tough.) In the final 15 minutes, squash some more beans against the side of the pot to thicken the juice. Add a little cayenne pepper if you like.

BARBECUE
⮞ SECRET ⮜
SMOKEY BEANS!

Your favorite baked bean recipe will take on a whole new dimension if you pop the open pot of beans into the smoker for about an hour over hickory wood (or whatever wood is going). This works especially well when doing ribs. While the ribs are wrapped in foil and finishing on the bottom rack, the beans can be smoking on the top rack.

ratatouille

Serves 8 as a side

The rich meatiness of barbecue is nicely offset by this classic European accompaniment. This recipe comes from my Franco-Canadian friend Michelle Allaire. It's best with lamb or pork.

1 eggplant, peel on, cut into 1-inch | 2.5-cm cubes

1 tsp. | 5 mL kosher salt

2 Tbsp. | 25 mL olive oil

4 cloves garlic, coarsely chopped

1 large onion (white or red), coarsely chopped

1 red or green bell pepper, cut into 1-inch | 2.5-cm dice

2 medium zucchinis, cut into 1-inch | 2.5-cm cubes

2 ripe plum tomatoes, coarsely chopped

kosher salt and freshly ground black pepper to taste

I Tbsp. | 15 mL fresh thyme or 1 tsp. | 5 mL dried thyme

1 Tbsp. | 15 mL fresh rosemary or 1 tsp. | 5 mL dried rosemary

Put the eggplant cubes into a colander and sprinkle them with the 1 tsp./5 mL of salt. Mix well and set over a bowl or in the sink for at least 2 hours. (Water will be drawn out of the eggplant, making it easier to cook without soaking up a lot of oil.)

Place 1 Tbsp./15 mL of the olive oil in a large skillet. Add the chopped garlic to the cold oil and turn the heat to medium, warming the pan slowly so the oil takes the flavor gradually. Add the onion and bell pepper and sauté until soft and shiny. Add the eggplant and the remaining 1 Tbsp./15 mL of oil. Sauté for a few minutes and then add the zucchini. Cook for at least 8 more minutes until all the vegetables are soft. Remove from the heat and transfer the mixture into a heavy pot. Place over medium heat and add the tomatoes. Season with salt and pepper and add the herbs. Bring to a boil, then turn the heat to low. Simmer uncovered for at least 1 hour, stirring frequently to allow the juices to reduce slightly. Serve hot or cold.

classic baked beans FOR A CROWD

Serves 14

This classic bean recipe, by friend and caterer Margie Gibb, is a perfect accompaniment to barbe-cued brisket or ribs, or just about anything else for that matter!

2 cups | 500 mL dried red kidney beans

2 cups | 500 mL dried cannellini or white kidney beans

2 cups | 500 mL dried black beans

1 lb. | 500 g double-smoked bacon, cut into large dice

2 large onions cut into 1/4-inch | 5-mm dice

4 cloves garlic, minced

1 Tbsp. | 15 mL chili powder

1 tsp. | 5 mL freshly ground cumin

2 tsp. | 10 mL finely chopped canned chipotles in adobe sauce

1¼ cups | 300 mL packed dark brown sugar

3 Tbsp. | 45 mL mild-flavored molasses

2 12-ounce | 342-mL bottles dark beer

kosher salt and freshly ground black pepper to taste

Pick over the beans to remove any stray pebbles and rinse. Place in a large saucepan, cover with cold water by 2 inches / 5 cm and bring to a rapid boil for 2 minutes. Cover, remove from the heat, and let stand for 1 hour. Drain the beans, and place them in a large Dutch oven or flameproof pot and set aside. (If you are short of time, rinsed canned beans work just as well—use 1 14-oz./398-mL can per cup/250 mL of dried beans.)

Cook the bacon in a heavy skillet until crisp. Remove the bacon and set aside.

Pour off all but 3 Tbsp./45 mL of the rendered bacon fat. Add the onions and cook over low to medium heat, stirring, until they are soft but not brown, about 10 minutes. (If you are short of bacon fat, add olive oil as necessary.)

Add the garlic, chili powder, cumin, and chipotles to the onion mixture; cook a further 5 minutes until the flavors are well blended. Add the onion mixture, sugar, molasses and beer to the beans and bring to a boil.

Reduce the heat to medium, and cook, covered, stirring occasionally, until the beans are soft and most of the liquid is absorbed, about 2 to 2 1/2 hours. Season with salt and pepper. Serve hot.

This dish improves if prepared one day in advance. Refrigerate overnight and then gently reheat.

SUPERCHARGED **corn on the cob** with savory butters

Allow one whole cob per guest

Almost nothing goes better with grilled or barbecued meat than good old corn on the cob, and it's so easy on the grill. It's also easy to do a little bit more to give it an extra jolt of buttery flavor.

1 unshucked ear of corn per guest

savory butter or butters (see below)

kosher salt

Soak the whole, unshucked corn in cold water for an hour. Remove from the water and place on a covered charcoal or gas grill over direct high heat. Cook for about half an hour, turning once or twice. Don't worry if the husks turn brown or black—the corn inside will be protected. Remove from the grill, let cool enough to handle, remove husks and serve with herbed butter and kosher salt. (If you want a more rustic, charred look and flavor, husk the corn cobs and grill them naked for 10 or 15 minutes, watching to make sure they char but don't burn.)

Four Great Savory Butters

Once you've made savory butters you'll always want to keep some in the freezer. Brought to room temperature, they are incredible on roasted corn on the cob or slathered on cornbread, and a pat of flavored butter on a freshly grilled steak or fish fillet is divine. You can even use it as a sautéing butter for thinly sliced mushrooms or scrambled eggs, or toss with some cooked noodles for a quick, easy side.

Mediterranean Herbed Butter

1 lb. | 500 g unsalted butter, at room temperature

4 Tbsp. | 60 mL finely chopped flatleaf Italian parsley

4 Tbsp. | 60 mL finely chopped fresh dill, basil or mint (or any combination of fresh herbs—try chervil, tarragon, sage, rosemary, etc.)

kosher salt to taste

BARBECUE ⤳ SECRET ⤜

Roasted corn is excellent with plain soft butter and a sprinkling of a simple rub consisting of one part kosher salt and one part ancho chile powder.

Red Pepper Butter

1/2 lb. | 250 g unsalted butter, at room temperature.

1 red bell pepper, roasted, peeled, seeded and coarsely chopped

1 tsp. | 5 mL paprika

kosher salt to taste

Garlic Chive Butter

1/2 lb. | 250 g unsalted butter, at room temperature

4 cloves garlic, put through a garlic press
(or double the amount of roasted garlic cloves, squeezed out of their skins)

2 Tbsp. | 25 mL finely chopped fresh chives

kosher salt to taste

Gorgonzola Butter

1/4 lb. | 125 g unsalted butter, at room temperature

3/4 cup | 175 mL Gorgonzola cheese

1 tsp. | 5 mL fresh lemon juice

kosher salt to taste

Cut the butter into cubes and place in a food processor. Add the flavoring ingredients and whiz until thoroughly blended. If you're serving it right away with corn, or on a piece of grilled meat, just place in a small bowl and serve.

If you want to store it, use a spatula to transfer the butter onto a sheet of waxed paper or plastic wrap and shape it into a rough cylinder. Fold the wrap around the butter and shape it into an even cylinder about 1¹/2 inches/4 cm in diameter. Twist the ends so the tube is sealed and tight, and seal both ends with a twist tie. Refrigerate or freeze until you need it. To serve, slice off disks of butter to dress steaks or corn, or to stuff inside a burger.

CURRIED **vegetables**

Serves 4

Serve this simple curry ladled over steamed basmati rice along with Tikka–Style Chicken Kebabs (see page 134).

2 Tbsp. | 25 mL vegetable oil

1 medium onion, peeled, quartered and separated into bite-size pieces

1 red bell pepper, cut into bite-size chunks

kosher salt to taste

2 cloves garlic, chopped

1/2 Tbsp. | 25 mL grated fresh ginger

2 Tbsp. | 25 mL curry powder

1 Tbsp. | 15 mL curry paste

1 cup | 250 mL broccoli florets

1 cup | 250 mL cauliflower florets

1 14-oz. | 398-mL can coconut milk

1 tsp. | 5 mL brown sugar

1 Tbsp. | 15 mL cornstarch

1/2 cup | 125 mL cold water

1/2 cup | 125 mL chopped cilantro

1 lime

cilantro sprigs, for garnish

Heat the oil in a cast iron skillet or nonstick frying pan over medium heat. Add the onion and bell pepper along with a pinch of salt. Toss for about 3 minutes or until the vegetables start to brown and soften. Add the garlic and ginger and sauté for another 1 or 2 minutes, taking care not to burn them. Add the curry powder and quickly stir for just half a minute or so to toast the spices. Add the curry paste, broccoli, cauliflower, coconut milk and brown sugar, mixing everything together. Bring to a boil, cover, and simmer for 10 or 15 minutes or until the vegetables are tender.

Mix the cornstarch with the cold water and swirl it into the pan, stirring constantly until the mixture thickens and turns glossy. Toss in the cilantro and squeeze in the juice of half a lime. Stir and serve, garnished with cilantro sprigs and remaining lime.

dilled LEMONY rice

Serves 8

This sticky, fragrant rice is a great accompaniment to just about anything.

2 Tbsp. | 25 mL butter

1 shallot, finely chopped

4 cups | 1 L homemade or canned low-salt chicken stock

2 cups | 500 mL short-grain rice

zest of 2 lemons, finely chopped

juice of 1 lemon

1/4 cup | 50 mL chopped fresh baby dill

1/2 tsp. | 2 mL kosher salt

1/4 tsp. | 1 mL black or white pepper

fresh dill fronds and lemon wedges, for garnish

Heat half the butter in a sauté pan over low-medium heat, add the shallot and cook until soft, stirring frequently, about 2 minutes. Set aside. In a saucepan over high heat bring the stock to a boil. Add the rice and return to a boil. Just as the stock begins to boil, reduce the heat to low. Add the shallot, lemon zest, dill, salt and pepper and remaining butter. Gently stir to evenly distribute all the ingredients. Cover the saucepan and cook for 15 minutes. Add the lemon juice, gently fluff with a fork, transfer to a serving bowl, garnish with dill and lemon and serve.

potato GALETTES

Serves 1

This is the perfect accompaniment to a grilled steak. The bed of crispy fried potatoes soaks up the juice from the steak and adds a sweet counterpoint to the savory meat. My kids love eating galettes as a fancy weekend breakfast, peeling off the potato petals and dipping them in ketchup.

1 medium-sized potato

2 to 4 Tbsp. | 25 to 60 mL cooking oil

kosher salt and freshly ground black pepper to taste

Peel the potato. With a mandoline or other slicing utensil (a good sharp chef's knife will do), slice the potato into paper-thin rounds. Over medium heat, preheat a small nonstick sauté pan and add 2 Tbsp./25 mL of the oil. With the oil fragrant but not smoking, start laying the potato rounds into the pan, starting from the outside and layering in concentric circles until the entire bottom of the pan is covered with what looks like the petals of a big flower. Place a second layer of potatoes over the first. Gently fry over medium heat until the bottom layer is golden brown. Carefully turn the galette, flipping it away from you to avoid spattering yourself with hot oil. Salt the browned side of the galette and cook the other side, adding more oil as needed. When the second side is nicely browned, turn onto some paper towels to drain the extra oil. Season the galette with salt and pepper and transfer to a warmed plate. Keep warm up for up to 1 hour in a 200°F/95°C oven. These are SO good!

dilled SMASHED potatoes

Serves 4 to 6

Fresh dill and nutmeg enhance the sweetness of the butter and potatoes in this classic dish. This is true comfort food that goes well with any kind of grilled meat or fish. If you are a garlic lover, squeeze in a few cloves of roasted garlic or sprinkle in some granulated garlic before mashing.

2 lbs. | 1 kg red nugget potatoes

1/2 cup | 125 mL butter, at room temperature

1 tsp. | 5 mL granulated onion

1/4 tsp. | 1 mL freshly grated nutmeg

2 Tbsp. | 25 mL chopped fresh dill

pinch cayenne

roasted garlic (optional) (see page 73)

kosher salt and freshly ground black pepper to taste

Trim any blemishes from the potatoes, leaving the skins on, and cut them in halves or quarters so you have 2-inch / 5-cm chunks. Place the potatoes in a large pot of cold water and bring to a boil over high heat. Reduce the heat to medium and boil for 10 to 15 minutes, or until a fork goes easily through a chunk of potato. Drain and return to the pot, reducing the heat to low. Add the butter, granulated onion, nutmeg, dill, cayenne and roasted garlic, if you like. Mash the potatoes just until they are half-mashed. Season with salt and pepper and serve immediately.

rich Italian HOBO PACKS

Serves 4

I don't know if there is any such thing as a rich Italian hobo, but if there were, this is what he would eat for dinner. My brother Allan perfected this truly decadent way to make roasted potatoes, and I have adapted the recipe for the grill. These are spectacular with grilled pork or chicken. The sage gives them extra depth of flavor.

4 Tbsp. | 60 mL olive oil

20 sage leaves

3 oz. | 100 g pancetta chopped into 1/4-inch | 5-mm pieces

2 leeks, rinsed well and thinly sliced (green parts removed)

1 clove garlic, peeled and finely sliced

1 lb. | 500 g yellow-fleshed potatoes,
peeled and cut into 1/2-inch | 1-cm slices

kosher salt and freshly ground black pepper to taste

1/2 cup | 125 mL whipping cream

1/2 cup | 125 mL Gorgonzola cheese

1/4 cup | 50 mL freshly grated Parmesan cheese

Prepare the grill for medium direct cooking (this is perfect if you are using the other side of a gas grill to cook a roast over indirect heat). Tear off four rectangular sheets of extra-wide foil and fold them in half so the foil is doubled. Brush the foil with olive oil. Divide the sage leaves evenly and place them on the oiled foil sheets. Add a layer of pancetta, then the leek and garlic slices, then the potato slices. Season with salt and pepper.

In a food processor combine the cream, Gorgonzola and all the Parmesan except for 1 Tbsp./15 mL. Whiz together until thoroughly mixed. Spoon equal dollops of the creamy mixture over the potatoes in each hobo pack. Gather the foil up around the ingredients and seal them tight enough so they won't leak, but loose enough so that some smoke will penetrate the packages.

Cook over direct medium heat for about half an hour. Open the hobo packs and sprinkle with the reserved Parmesan. For informal dining, just put the hobo packs on the plates and let your guests spoon out the contents themselves.

linguine with gorgonzola CREAM SAUCE

Serves 2 as a main, 4 as an appetizer, 6 as a side

This is the fastest, and the most luxurious, pasta sauce I know. It's great next to a grilled steak, chop, or chicken breast or as a first course. If you're serving it as an appetizer, avoid big portions—this is filling!

1 lb. | 500 g fresh plain or spinach-flavored fettuccine

1/4 lb. | 125 g Gorgonzola cheese, crumbled

1/2 cup | 125 mL whipping cream

2 Tbsp. | 25 mL unsalted butter, at room temperature

1/4 cup | 50 mL freshly grated Parmigiano-Reggiano cheese

Throw the fresh fettucine into a big pot of boiling salted water. Place the gorgonzola, cream and butter in a saucepan and cook over low-medium heat, stirring constantly, until the ingredients are combined into a smooth creamy sauce. When the pasta is cooked as you like it, drain, toss with the sauce and sprinkle with the grated Parmeggiano-Reggiano. Serve immediately on warm plates.

LATIN-STYLE rice AND black beans

Serves 4 to 8 depending on what you're serving with it

I have adapted this recipe from Chris Schlesinger and John Willoughby's *Licence to Grill* by adding some red bell pepper and a little powdered ancho chile. It's an excellent all-purpose accompaniment that goes with just about anything, particularly any dish with Latin flavor influences.

2 Tbsp. | 25 mL olive oil

1 small yellow onion, minced

1 Tbsp. | 15 mL minced garlic

1/2 red bell pepper, cut into 1/4-inch | 5-mm dice

1/2 jalapeño, minced

1 tsp. | 5 mL toasted cumin seeds

1 tsp. | 5 mL ground ancho chile

1 cup ¦ 250 mL long-grain rice

1²/₃ cups | 400 mL water

1 tsp. | 5 mL kosher salt

1 cup | 250 mL cooked black beans or canned black beans,
drained and rinsed

1/2 cup | 125 mL roughly chopped cilantro

kosher salt and freshly ground black pepper to taste

Heat 1 Tbsp./15 mL of the oil in a large skillet over medium heat until hot but not smoking. Add the onion and sauté for 3 or 4 minutes, stirring occasionally. Add the garlic, bell pepper, jalepeño, cumin seeds and ground ancho and continue to cook for another 2 minutes, stirring occasionally. Add the rice, the remaining 1 Tbsp./15 mL of oil, and cook for 1 more minute until the rice is shiny and slightly translucent. Add the water and salt and bring just to a simmer, then reduce the heat to medium-low. Cover and cook until the water is absorbed and the rice is tender, about 15 minutes.

When the rice is cooked, add the beans, mix well, and cook for about 5 minutes, stirring occasionally, to heat the beans through. Add the cilantro, season with salt and pepper, stir well, and you're ready to serve.

tidewater COLESLAW

Serves 8 to 10

My dear friend and fellow Butt Shredder Kathy Richardier discovered this slaw many years ago and I have substituted my favorite toasted cumin seeds for the celery seeds in the original recipe. This pungent, high-sugar slaw is best as a condiment, piled high on top of a pulled pork sandwich or burger, or on the side of a few slices of barbecued brisket.

1¹/₂ cups | 375 mL mayonnaise

1/2 cup | 125 mL white vinegar

1/3 cup | 75 mL white sugar

1 Tbsp. | 15 mL toasted cumin seeds

1 small head cabbage, finely shredded

2 carrots, peeled and finely grated

Whisk the mayonnaise, vinegar, sugar and cumin together in a bowl. Toss with the cabbage and carrots and refrigerate. You can make this slaw a few hours ahead of time. Toss it just before serving to redistribute the dressing.

goober SLAW

Serves 8 to 10

My old pal Ian "Big Daddy" Baird was kind enough to share this crunchy, nutty slaw recipe with me.

1¹/₄ cups | 300 mL aïoli (see page 73)
or good store-bought mayonnaise

1/3 cup | 75 mL apple cider vinegar

1/3 cup | 75 mL sugar

2 Tbsp. | 25 mL milk

1 clove garlic, finely minced

1/2 tsp. | 2 mL celery salt

1 small head cabbage, finely grated

2 carrots, peeled and finely grated

3/4 cup | 175 mL chopped, salted dry-roast peanuts

Put the aïoli or mayonnaise, vinegar, sugar, milk, garlic and celery salt in a container with a secure lid and shake until well blended. Combine the cabbage and carrots. Pour the dressing over the coleslaw, toss and refrigerate for an hour. Just before serving add the peanuts and toss again.

field greens WITH WALNUT OIL and toasted pumpkin seeds

Serves 4

Walnut oil is expensive, but a little goes a long way. It perfectly offsets the bitterness of the greens and brings out the nuttiness of the pumpkin seeds in this simple, elegant salad. Serve it as a side salad, garnish a burger with it, or put a pile under a grilled steak.

1/4 cup | 50 mL pumpkin seeds

3 cups | 750 mL mesclun greens, fresh arugula,
fresh watercress or a combo

1 bunch fresh basil, stems removed and leaves
gently torn in half

2 Tbsp. | 25 mL toasted walnut oil

1 crisp apple, peeled, cored and cut
into 1/2-inch | 1-cm chunks

1/2 tsp. | 2 mL kosher or Maldon salt, or to taste

freshly ground black pepper to taste

lemon wedges, for garnish

Toast the pumpkin seeds in a dry frying pan over medium heat or under a broiler until they start popping and turning light brown. Set aside to cool. Place the greens in a salad bowl, add the walnut oil, pumpkin seeds, apple chunks, salt and a few grindings of pepper. Toss thoroughly. Garnish with lemon.

rice, ASPARAGUS and cucumber SALAD

Serves 8

This is a slight adaptation of a recipe in a 1994 *Bon Appétit* magazine. The salad tastes like summer itself. You cannot make it once without making it again and again.

1 3/4 cups | 425 mL water

1 cup | 250 mL long-grain white rice

1 pound | 500 g asparagus, trimmed and cut into 1-inch | 2.5-cm pieces

1 1/2 cups | 375 mL long English cucumber chopped into 1/4-inch | 5-mm dice

1/2 cup | 125 mL chopped chives

2 Tbsp. | 25 mL Dijon mustard

1 Tbsp. | 15 mL honey

1 Tbsp. | 15 mL white wine vinegar

1/2 tsp. | 2 mL dry mustard

2 1/2 Tbsp. | 40 mL vegetable oil

1/4 cup | 50 mL chopped fresh dill

1 tsp. | 5 mL finely minced lemon zest

kosher salt and freshly ground black pepper to taste

green leaf or butter lettuce

dill sprigs, for garnish

Bring the water to a boil in a medium saucepan over high heat. Add the rice and return to a boil. Reduce the heat to low, cover and cook for about 20 minutes. Place the rice in a bowl, fluff it with a fork, and let it cool to room temperature.

Blanch the asparagus in boiling salted water for 1 or 2 minutes, just until it is bright green and still slightly crisp. Plunge the asparagus in a bowl of cold water to stop the cooking process. Drain and pat dry. Add the asparagus, cucumber and chives to the rice.

Combine the Dijon mustard, honey, vinegar and dry mustard in a small bowl. Gradually mix in the oil and then mix in the dill and lemon zest. Mix the dressing with the salad mixture. Season with salt and pepper. Line a large bowl with lettuce and mound the salad in the bowl. Garnish with dill sprigs.

potato SALAD ADOBO

Serves 6 to 8

This Southwestern take on potato salad is a perfect side dish and makes a great potluck contribution to someone else's barbecue!

2 lbs. | 1 kg small red potatoes

2 Tbsp. | 25 mL olive oil

1 medium onion, finely minced

1/2 cup | 125 mL cider vinegar

2 Tbsp. | 25 mL sugar

2 chipotles in adobo sauce, seeded and finely chopped

1 cup | 250 mL mayonnaise

1 tsp. | 5 mL toasted sesame oil

2 green onions, chopped

2 Tbsp. | 25 mL chopped cilantro

1 roasted red bell pepper, roughly chopped

kosher salt and freshly ground black pepper

1/2 cup | 125 mL toasted pecans, roughly chopped

cilantro sprigs, for garnish

Cook the potatoes in a large pot of lightly salted water until just tender. Drain and set aside.

In a heavy skillet over medium heat, heat the olive oil and cook the onions until soft but not brown, about 6 minutes. Add the vinegar and sugar to the skillet, stir to dissolve the sugar and remove from the heat.

In a food processor, combine the chipotles, mayonnaise and sesame oil and blend till smooth. Cut the still-warm potatoes into halves or quarters and add to the vinegar/onion mixture, tossing so the potatoes absorb the vinegar. Add the flavored mayonnaise, green onions, cilantro and roasted bell pepper, tossing to coat everything. Season with salt and pepper, toss one last time, transfer to a serving bowl and top with the toasted pecans and cilantro sprigs.

asian NOODLE salad WITH SESAME MAYONNAISE

Serves 3 to 4

This is a great summer salad that goes well with grilled chicken or beside any Asian-flavored grilled or barbecued meat. I like to use rice spaghetti noodles (as opposed to Asian rice vermicelli, which doesn't have the same chewiness). You can find rice spaghetti noodles in health food stores, but plain old durum wheat spaghetti also works well.

For the mayonnaise

1 cup | 250 mL mayonnaise

1 tsp. | 5 mL toasted sesame oil

1/2 tsp. | 2 mL soy sauce (or to taste)

1 tsp. | 5 mL Chinese chili sauce or spicy Szechuan chili oil (or to taste)

1 Tbsp. | 15 mL grated fresh lemon, lime or orange rind

For the salad

1 16 oz. | 454 g package rice or wheat spaghetti noodles

2 Tbsp. | 25 mL chopped cilantro

1 to 2 Tbsp. | 15 to 25 mL toasted sesame seeds (to taste)

2 fresh limes, cut into wedges

Combine the dressing ingredients and refrigerate for at least a few hours or overnight.

In a large pot of boiling salted water, cook the noodles for 8 to 10 minutes or until al dente. Drain the noodles and rinse with cold water. Drain again thoroughly. Toss with the sesame mayo, cilantro and sesame seeds. Serve garnished with lime wedges.

MIMI'S tabouleh (COUSCOUS salad)

Serves 8 as a side

This recipe from friend Michelle Allaire uses instant couscous, which is moistened by all the juices that come out of the vegetables as they sit with the grain in the fridge. It is usually served as a side with lamb but can be an attractive alternative main course for a vegetarian guest. To "beef" it up, add blanched green beans, blanched carrots and cooked chick peas.

1 package (about 10 oz. | 300 g) instant couscous

4 green onions, thinly sliced

1 Tbsp. | 15 mL red onion cut into 1/4-inch | 5-mm dice

1 cup | 250 mL long English cucumber cut into
1/4-inch | 5-mm dice

1/2 red or green bell pepper, cut into 1/4-inch | 5-mm dice

1 cup | 250 mL fresh tomato cut into 1/4-inch | 5-mm dice

1 cup | 250 mL chopped fresh parsley

1 Tbsp. | 15 mL finely chopped fresh mint

1 tsp. | 5 mL kosher salt

1/2 tsp. | 10 mL freshly ground black pepper

1 Tbsp. | 15 mL ground cumin

freshly squeezed juice of 2 lemons

1 cup | 250 mL good-quality extra virgin olive oil

Pour the entire packet of uncooked couscous into a large bowl. Add the remaining ingredients, mix well and let sit in the fridge for at least 4 hours. Remove from the fridge at least 1 hour before serving. Mix again, taste and adjust the seasoning and oil to taste.

corn muffins WITH ROASTED pecans

Makes 12 muffins

The rich, mild nuttiness of toasted pine nuts and chewy texture of the roasted corn kernels make these slightly sweet corn muffins, based on a recipe by Southwestern food guru Mark Miller, the perfect side. Try them with barbecued meat, chili or scrambled eggs ... and don't skimp on the butter!

vegetable cooking spray

3/4 cup | 175 mL pecans (about 4$\frac{1}{2}$ ounces)

2/3 cup | 150 mL fresh or thawed frozen corn kernels

1$\frac{1}{2}$ cups | 375 mL unbleached all-purpose flour

1$\frac{1}{2}$ cups | 375 mL cornmeal

1/3 cup | 75 mL sugar

1 Tbsp. | 15 mL baking powder

3/4 tsp. | 4 mL kosher salt

3 large eggs, separated

1$\frac{1}{2}$ cups | 375 mL milk

1/3 cup | 75 mL honey

1/4 cup plus 2 Tbsp. | 75 mL unsalted butter, melted

2 Tbsp. | 25 mL chopped fresh thyme (optional)

Preheat the oven to 375°F/190°C. Grease a 12-cup muffin pan with the cooking spray. Toast the pine nuts on a baking sheet until golden brown, about 3 or 4 minutes. Transfer to a plate and cool. Cook the corn in a skillet over low heat, stirring often, until browned and slightly dry, 6 to 8 minutes. Transfer to a plate to cool.

In a large bowl, mix together the flour, cornmeal, sugar, baking powder and salt. In another bowl, beat the egg whites until stiff but not dry. In another bowl, combine the egg yolks, milk, honey and melted butter and mix thoroughly. Make a well in the middle of the dry ingredients and pour in the milk mixture along with the pine nuts and corn; stir just to combine. Fold in the beaten egg whites and herbs. Spoon the batter into the prepared pan and bake for 20 to 25 minutes, until a toothpick or knife blade comes out clean. Let cool for a few minutes in the pan, then turn onto a cooling rack.

coconut JOHNNYCAKES

Serves 8

I have replaced the milk in a classic Johnnycake recipe with coconut milk and added shredded coconut for an interesting texture. The addition of dried chili flakes and lime zest offsets the sweetness. This is great as a side with Asian-flavored main dishes, or as a savory-sweet dessert square with a drizzle of honey.

1/2 cup | 125 mL melted butter

1/4 cup | 50 mL sugar

1 egg

1½ cups | 375 mL best-quality coconut milk
(use light if you are worried about clogging your arteries)

3/4 cup | 175 mL all-purpose flour

1/4 cup | 50 mL medium shredded coconut

1 cup | 250 mL coarse-ground cornmeal

2½ tsp. | 12 mL baking powder

1/2 tsp. | 2 mL kosher salt

zest of 1 lime, finely chopped

1 tsp. | 5 mL dried hot chili flakes

Preheat the oven to 350°F/175°C. Grease an 8-inch/2 L square pan. In a food processor, combine the butter, sugar and egg and whiz until smooth. With the processor on, pour in the coconut milk and blend until incorporated into the mixture.

Combine the flour, coconut, cornmeal, baking powder and salt in a large bowl. Make a well in the center and pour in the wet ingredients, adding the lime zest and chili flakes just before you stir. Stir until the ingredients are just barely combined. Pour the batter into the prepared pan and bake in the center of the oven for 30 to 35 minutes or until a toothpick or knife comes out clean.

COWBOY cornbread

Serves 6 to 8

This recipe is a meal in itself, but is also a great side dish. I adapted it from a recipe that my Texan friend Amy shared with me.

1$\frac{1}{2}$ cups | 375 mL cornmeal

1/2 tsp. | 2 mL baking soda

2 eggs

1 can (16 oz. | 500 mL) cream-style corn

1 tsp. | 5 mL kosher salt

1 cup | 250 mL milk

1/4 cup | 50 mL olive oil

1 cup | 250 mL Mark's Otherworldly Taco Filling (see page 77)

2 Tbsp. | 25 mL cornmeal

1 cup | 250 mL chopped onion

1 medium green bell pepper, chopped

3 jalapeño peppers, chopped

1 jar (2 oz. | 57 mL) pimentos, chopped

1/2 lb. | 250 g grated Cheddar cheese

Preheat the oven to 350°F/180°C. Mix the 1$\frac{1}{2}$ cups/375 mL cornmeal, soda, eggs, corn, salt, milk and oil together. Set aside. Warm up the taco filling in a skillet. Sprinkle the 2 Tbsp./25 mL cornmeal in the bottom of the greased baking dish. Pour in half the cornbread batter. Layer the taco filling, onion, green pepper, jalapeños, pimentos and grated cheese. Top with the remaining cornbread batter. Bake for 60 to 70 minutes. Cool for at least 5 minutes before serving.

grilled RICE cakes

Serves 3 to 5

These traditional Japanese rice cakes are often found, stuffed with tuna or salmon, in Japanese take-out shops. They take on a wonderful, crunchy, chewy texture when grilled and go well with any Asian-flavored grilled or barbecued meat. I learned how to make them from Vancouver chef Trevor Hooper's cookbook, *Asian Tapas and Wild Sushi*. You can get sushi rice at just about any super-market these days. If you can't find it there, look for an Asian market or gourmet food store.

3 cups | 750 mL sushi rice

3³/4 cups | 925 mL water

neutral-flavored oil, like peanut or canola

Teriyaki Sauce (see page 63)

Place the rice and water in a medium pot and bring to a boil over high heat. Boil for 2 minutes, cover and reduce the heat to medium. Cook for another 5 minutes, reduce the heat to low and cook for 15 more minutes. Do not remove the lid. Turn off the heat and let the covered pot stand for another 10 minutes.

Empty the rice into a bowl and let stand for 5 minutes or until it's cool enough to handle with your bare hands. Have a bowl of cold water handy to wet your hands before you form each rice cake.

Wet your hands and grab about 1/2 cup / 125 mL of rice. Press it firmly, cupping your hands to shape the rice into a triangular shape about the size of a wedge of pie. Squeeze it tightly so it will stick together well when it's grilled. Once you have formed all the rice into about 10 neat wedges, the rice cakes can be covered and refrigerated for up to a day or two before grilling.

To cook, use a basting brush to paint each rice cake with oil. Grill over direct high heat until they are crisp and golden brown with nice char marks. Drizzle each rice cake with teriyaki sauce. Allow at least 2 per person.

The Burger Connection

Chapter V

he rest of this book is organized under categories relating to specific kinds of meat or seafood, but for backyard cooks the burger is in a category all its own. Today the hamburger is ubiquitous. There's almost no menu without one, and the range of burgers available in restaurants ranges from the cheap and tasteless cardboard abominations of the fast food chains to the outrageous $40 foie gras, truffle and short-rib-stuffed burgers of New York's trendiest kitchens. Just as we have traced the origins of barbecue to European immigrants to America, we can follow the roots of the modern hamburger back to, well, Hamburg, Germany, where cheap cuts of beef were chopped, seasoned and served cooked or raw to the lower classes. The "Hamburg Steak" first appeared on New York menus in the mid-1800s, and by the end of the nineteenth century it was served in restaurants as far away as Walla Walla, WA. It's a lot harder to determine who had the idea to create a sandwich out of that chopped beef steak to create the burger we know and love today—there are at least five different claims ranging from Wisconsin to Texas. But what we do know is that the hamburger made a successful leap from the restaurant kitchen to the backyard grill, and everyone knows who makes the best burgers in the world —your Dad, of course! Until now, that is. Armed with this short but powerful collection of burger recipes I guarantee you will become a legend in your own mind—and maybe even in your entire neighborhood! Whether you cook the simplest Dadburger or the most exotic Oyster Burger, you'll find something here to sink your teeth into!

Chicken Wings—Fiery Southwestern and Lemon Dijon Rosemary
page 142

Kate's Tasty Asian Chicken Thighs served with Asian Noodle Salad with Sesame Mayonnaise and Grilled Asparagus

pages 138, 105, and 74

The King of Barbecue: Beef Brisket
page 150

Real Barbecued Ribs
page 124

classic dadburger DELUXE

Makes 12 to 16 patties, depending on how big you like them

This recipe will feed a crowd, or four teenagers. You can easily half this recipe. If your kids are like mine and don't like bits of onion and garlic in their burgers, substitute 1 tsp./5 mL each of granulated onion and granulated garlic for the fresh variety.

For the burger mix

6 lbs. | 2.7 kg medium ground beef
(or half-and-half ground beef and
ground pork)

1 medium onion, finely chopped

1 head roasted garlic, cloves
squeezed out and mashed with a fork

1 Tbsp. | 15 mL toasted sesame oil

2 Tbsp. | 25 mL dark soy sauce or
Worcestershire sauce or a combination

1/2 tsp. | 2 mL freshly grated nutmeg

1/4 tsp. | 1 mL cayenne
(or more if you like more heat)

lots of freshly ground black pepper

2 eggs

1/2 cup | 125 mL cold water

To finish the burgers

barbecue sauce

12 to 16 cheese slices (optional)

12 to 16 hamburger buns

Mix the burger ingredients together with your hands in a large nonreactive bowl. Wet your hands in cold water before you form the mixture into chunks the size of tennis-balls. Flatten them into patties, placing them on a cookie sheet lined with wax paper. Each patty will be about 1/2 lb./250 g before cooking. Place in the freezer for an hour to firm them up.

Preheat your grill for medium direct heat. Grill for 6 minutes per side or until they are springy to the touch, glazing with barbecue sauce. Top each patty with a slice of cheese for the last couple of minutes of cooking. Serve on buns with your favorite burger condiments.

asian chicken BURGER

Serves 4

This chicken burger has a light, fluffy texture and the kind of comfort-food taste we associate with take-out Chinese food. Serve with ice-cold Asian beer like Tsing-Tao, Kingfisher or Kirin.

For the sauce

1/2 cup | 125 mL mayonnaise

1/2 tsp. | 2 mL sesame oil

1 tsp. | 5 mL hot Asian chili sauce

juice of 1/2 lime

For the burger mix

1½ lbs. | 750 g freshly ground chicken

1 cup | 250 mL fresh bread crumbs

1/4 cup | 50 mL minced green onions

1/4 cup | 50 mL finely chopped cilantro

1 large egg, lightly beaten

1 Tbsp. | 15 mL oyster sauce

1 Tbsp. | 15 mL hoisin sauce

1 Tbsp. | 15 mL soy sauce

1 Tbsp. | 15 mL liquid honey

2 tsp. | 10 mL Dijon mustard

1 tsp. | 5 mL toasted sesame oil

1/2 tsp. | 2 mL kosher salt

1/2 tsp. | 2 mL freshly ground
black pepper

To finish the burgers

Asian Barbecue Sauce (page 68)

4 lettuce leaves

4 hamburger buns, lightly buttered and sprinkled
with granulated garlic

4 1/2-inch | 1-cm slices grilled pineapple (optional)

In a medium nonreactive bowl combine the mayo, sesame oil, chili sauce and lime juice. Cover and refrigerate (you can make this the day before).

Gently combine the burger ingredients, mixing with your hands. Wet your hands with cold water and shape the mixture into 4 patties that are 3/4 inch / 2 cm thick. Cover and refrigerate for at least 1 hour.

Brush the patties with olive oil and grill over direct medium heat until well done (the internal temperature will be 160°F/71°C), 5 to 6 minutes per side. Brush with barbecue sauce for the last few minutes of cooking, if you like. Transfer the burgers from the grill to a platter, tent with foil and let rest for 4 or 5 minutes. Meanwhile, lightly toast the buns on the grill. Generously slather the buns with the sauce, add the patties, top with some lettuce (or a slice of grilled pineapple, if you like) and serve.

kid-friendly TURKEY burgers

Makes 6 burgers

These burgers taste so much like real fast-food chicken nuggets you'll think you mechanically de-boned them yourself!

For the burger mix

2 lbs. | 1 kg ground turkey thigh meat

1 cup | 250 mL fresh bread crumbs

1 tsp. | 5 mL granulated garlic

1 tsp. | 5 mL onion salt

1/4 tsp. | 1 mL freshly grated nutmeg

1 tsp. | 5 mL freshly ground pepper

pinch cayenne

1 egg

To finish the burgers

Championship Barbecue Rub (page 51)

vegetable cooking spray

6 hamburger buns

Combine all the burger mix ingredients in a large bowl with your hands, being careful not to over-work. Shape into patties that are 1/2 inch/1 cm thick, wetting your hands first with cold water to prevent sticking. Place the burgers on a baking sheet lined with waxed paper.

Sprinkle the burger patties lightly with rub and spray them with the cooking spray. At this point it helps to refrigerate them for about 1/2 hour to firm them up a little. Prepare your grill for direct medium heat. Oil the grill and place the patties on it, rub side down. Sprinkle rub on the other side of the patties, close the grill and cook for 3 or 4 minutes per side or until the burgers are cooked through and springy to the touch. Serve immediately on soft burger buns with your favorite condiments.

Thai flavored BEEF burgers with sautéed shiitakes

Serves 4

This recipe, adapted from *Weber's Big Book of Grilling*, features lightly sautéed shiitakes and needs no further condiment to give your tastebuds a trip around the world.

For the burger mix

1½ lbs. | 750 g ground beef chuck (80 percent lean)

2 Tbsp. | 25 mL finely chopped fresh Thai or Italian basil

1 Tbsp. | 15 mL fresh lime juice

2 tsp. | 10 mL fish sauce

2 cloves garlic, finely minced

1 tsp. | 5 mL grated or finely chopped lime zest

1 tsp. | 5 mL grated fresh ginger

1/2 tsp. | 2 mL freshly ground black pepper

For the mushrooms

3 Tbsp. | 45 mL unsalted butter

2 Tbsp. | 25 mL canola or peanut oil

1 small shallot, finely chopped

2 tsp. | 10 mL grated fresh ginger

8 oz. | 250 g fresh shiitake mushrooms, stems removed, cut into 1/4-inch |5-mm slices

few drops sesame oil

1/4 tsp. | 1 mL kosher salt

1/4 tsp. | 1 mL freshly ground black pepper

To finish the burgers

4 hamburger buns, lightly buttered and sprinkled with granulated onion

1 tsp. | 15 mL toasted sesame seeds

In a large bowl gently mix the burger ingredients with your hands. Shape them into 4 patties about 3/4 inch/2 cm thick. Cover and refrigerate for at least 1/2 hour or up to 4 hours.

Prepare your grill for direct medium heat. While the grill is heating, prepare the mushrooms. In a sauté pan over medium heat, melt the butter with the oil and add the shallot and ginger. Add the mushrooms and cook, stirring occasionally, until tender, 4 to 6 minutes. Add the sesame oil, salt and pepper and mix thoroughly. Set aside and keep warm.

Brush the burger patties with oil and grill over direct medium heat for 4 to 5 minutes per side or until the internal temperature reaches 160°F/71°C. Remove from the heat. Grill the buns for about 30 to 60 seconds, butter side down, until nicely toasted.

Serve the hot burgers on the toasted buns, topped with the mushrooms and a sprinkling of sesame seeds.

beef BURGER WITH herbed butter core and caramelized onions

Serves 4

This recipe won the burger category at the Canadian National Barbecue Championship in Whistler, British Columbia, in the summer of 2003. More than a burger, it is the Atkins equivalent of a jelly doughnut (if you forego the bun). It's a life-shaping experience that should probably be accompanied by some kind of parental guidance message. Be careful to whom you serve this; your guests may stalk you until you cook it for them again.

1½ to 2 lbs. | 750 g to 1 kg of ground beef, 20 percent fat content

1/2 tsp. | 2 mL or so freshly grated nutmeg

4 1/2-inch | 1-cm disks of frozen Mediterranean Herbed Butter (page 90)

1 Tbsp. | 15 mL Dijon mustard

Championship Barbecue Rub (page 51)

4 hamburger buns

extra softened Herbed Butter for the buns

granulated garlic

1/2 cup | 125 mL chèvre (a creamy white French-style goat cheese), at room temperature

2 large roasted red bell peppers

Caramelized Onions (see following page)

In a nonreactive bowl, combine the beef and nutmeg. Mix together lightly with your hands, being careful not to overwork it. Split into 4 equal portions and roll into balls. Poke your thumb in the middle of each ball to create a hole and insert a frozen disk of herbed butter. Encase the butter in the burger as you shape it into a classic burger shape about 3/4 inch / 2 cm thick, ensuring that there are no openings where molten butter could run out.

Coat the burger patties lightly with mustard and sprinkle them with a light coating of the rub. Preheat your grill to medium heat. Either spray the burgers

Caramelized Onions (see following page)

A Library of Burger ⇝ Toppings ≺

We're all so used to iceberg lettuce, ketchup, mayo, ball-park mustard, green relish and sliced onion and tomato on our burgers that we hardly notice them any more. Try these unusual burger toppings for a change and experiment with your own combinations.

- thinly sliced button mushrooms sautéed with a smashed garlic clove in butter and olive oil

- crunchy–style peanut butter, bacon, raw onion and lettuce

- an egg fried in butter, over easy, with a leaf of iceberg lettuce and a slather of mayo

- avocado slices, bacon and salsa

- caramelized onion, roasted red pepper and goat cheese

- tomato slices, thinly sliced red onion and fresh arugula

- black olive paste and slices of hard-boiled egg

- Brie or Gorgonzola cheese

with vegetable oil spray or coat the grill with oil. Place the burgers on the grill and cook for about 4 or 5 minutes per side or until the patties become firm, but not hard, to the touch.

Remove the burgers from the grill, tent with foil and let rest for 4 or 5 minutes. In the meantime, coat the buns with the softened herbed butter, sprinkle with a little granulated garlic and toast for 30 to 60 seconds on your grill.

Dress the burgers with a slather of goat cheese, a piece of roasted red pepper and a dollop of caramelized onion. Inhale. (Note: warn your guests that the burgers have a molten filling or they could be in for a shock! In any case have plenty of napkins at the ready. These are very juicy burgers.)

caramelized onions

Makes about 1 cup | 250 mL

This makes a great topping for burgers but is an excellent all-purpose condiment. Try it as an omelette filling or a topping for grilled pork chops. Mix it with goat cheese and spread it on crackers for a tangy sweet appetizer.

2 Tbsp. | 25 mL butter, olive oil or a combination of both

4 medium onions, peeled and sliced into rings

1/2 tsp. | 2 mL kosher salt

1 tsp. | 5 mL sugar

1/2 tsp. | 2 mL ground cinnamon

pinch cayenne

In a large skillet heat the butter/olive oil over medium heat. Add the onions and salt and sauté until soft, about 5 minutes. Add the sugar, cinnamon and cayenne and continue to sauté, stirring regularly, until the onions are shiny and brown, about 15 minutes, being careful not to burn them (add a little water if necessary to prevent burning).

**BARBECUE
⤝ SECRETS ⤜**

For extra-juicy burgers, add some cold water (about 1 Tbsp. | 15 mL per lb. | 454 g) to your raw burger meat before you mix it. For extra-tender burgers, don't overwork the burger mix.

lamb burger WITH MOLTEN goat cheese core

Serves 4

We eat so much ground beef that we almost forget what beef tastes like. When you eat a lamb burger you actually taste the lamb and it makes for a deliciously different grilling experience. The goat cheese stuffing adds an orgiastic twist. Don't forget to freeze the goat cheese!

For the tzatziki

1 tsp. | 5 mL ground cumin

1 cup | 250 mL plain Greek full-fat yoghurt

1 Tbsp. | 15 mL finely chopped fresh mint leaves

1/3 long English cucumber, finely grated

To finish the burgers

Mediterranean Herbed Butter (page 90)

2 large fresh rounds of pita bread

fresh sliced tomatoes

1/2 red onion, very thinly sliced

1 bunch fresh arugula, washed and dried

For the patties

1 1/2 lbs. | 750 g ground lamb

2 Tbsp. | 25 mL chopped fresh mint

1 tsp. | 5 mL dried oregano

1/2 tsp. | 2 mL kosher salt

freshly ground black pepper to taste

3 oz. | 75 g soft goat cheese (chèvre), frozen and sliced into 4 1/2-inch | 1-cm disks

2 Tbsp. | 25 mL softened Mediterranean Herbed Butter (page 90)

kosher salt and freshly ground black pepper to taste

To make the tzatziki, dry-fry the ground cumin over medium heat for 30 seconds or until it becomes fragrant and browns just slightly. Transfer the cumin from the hot pan into a bowl. Add the yoghurt, mint and cucumber, mix thoroughly, cover and refrigerate until needed.

With your hands, gently mix the lamb with the mint, oregano, salt and a few grindings of pepper. Divide into 4 equal portions and shape into balls. Make a hole in each patty with your thumb and insert a disc of frozen goat cheese. Carefully seal the hole and shape the ball into a patty 3/4 inch / 2 cm thick, being sure to cover the cheese with the meat. Season the outside of the patties with salt and pepper. Lightly brush the patties with olive oil and grill over medium direct heat for 4 to 5 minutes per side or until the internal temperature is 160°F/71°C.

Take the burgers off the grill and spread a thin layer of the herbed butter on the top of each (if you don't have any herbed butter, drizzle them with a little olive oil—just enough to make them glisten). Let rest for 3 or 4 minutes.

Just before you're ready to serve, toast the pitas on the grill for 10 or 15 seconds per side. Cut the pitas in half, open them up and stuff the burgers inside. Dress with the tomatoes, onion, arugula and tzatziki.

the Wakefield Inn OYSTER burger

Serves 4

Years ago the Wakefield Inn, a pub on BC's Sunshine Coast, invented the ultimate burger. Ironically, it's not grilled. To get the right texture you need to pan-fry the oysters. The Wakefield Inn uses seasoned flour, but I prefer the extra crunch of cornmeal. Serve with a dill pickle, a dollop of Potato Salad Adobo (page 104) and a big mug of cold beer.

1 tsp. | 5 mL ground cumin

1 tsp. | 5 mL ground ancho chiles

1 tsp. | 5 mL freshly ground black pepper

1/2 cup | 125 mL cornmeal

1 Tbsp. | 15 mL butter

1 Tbsp. | 15 mL olive oil

12 medium/large fresh West Coast oysters

4 burger buns, toasted and buttered

4 Tbsp. | 60 mL commercial tartar sauce
(or Chipotle and Roasted Garlic Aïoli, page 73)

1 bunch green leaf lettuce

4 slices crisply cooked bacon

1 thinly sliced ripe tomato

pickle slice and parsley sprigs, for garnish

Combine the cumin, ground ancho, pepper and cornmeal and pour the mixture on a dinner plate. Heat the butter and oil in a heavy skillet over medium-high heat until the butter is sizzling. Lightly coat the oysters in the cornmeal mixture and fry in the oil and butter until crisp on the outside and done inside, about 2 to 3 minutes per side.

On each toasted and buttered bun spread 1 Tbsp./15 mL of tartar sauce. Add a leaf or two of lettuce, 3 of the fried oysters, one crispy slice of bacon (ripped in half) and 1 or 2 slices of tomato. Sprinkle with salt and pepper. Top with the other half bun, garnish with pickle and a parsley sprig.

The Meat of the Matter

M

Chapter VI

PORK

There was a time in the 1990s when pork producers decided that the public wanted to avoid fatty foods, so they fed and bred their hogs to a point where they were competing with skinless chicken breasts for a place on the diet-conscious yuppie's plate. They had forgotten one of the most profound barbecue secrets of all, the formula that says: FOOD + FAT = FLAVOR

And of all the fats, pork fat is one of the most flavorful. Thank goodness the North American palate has come to its senses and richer foods are once again socially acceptable. Pork producers have responded to this positive trend by offering cuts of pork that are worth eating again. When you choose pork at your local butcher shop or in the supermarket, look for nice lines of creamy fat around the meat and a rich, marbled texture in the muscle itself. Fat is what literally creates the sizzle when you grill, and without it your barbecued pork would taste like cardboard.

Fat is not only flavorful, it is supremely nutritious. Pig meat fed North American's earliest settlers, and as an inexpensive source of energy-packed protein it has always been a staple of working folks everywhere. And, of course, pork is the lead player on the competitive barbecue stage and the image of the happy pig is synonymous with barbecue culture. All hail the mighty pig, provider to us all!

real BARBECUED RIBS

Serves 2 to 4

To get the taste of authentic barbecued ribs you need to cook them slowly the traditional way, in a water smoker or barbecue pit at a low temperature. This is how we do ribs in competition. You can also accomplish something close to this using indirect low heat on your covered charcoal or gas grill.

2 racks pork side ribs, St. Louis cut
(with the breast plate attached)

2 Tbsp. | 25 mL prepared mustard

1 tsp. | 5 mL or so granulated garlic

1/2 cup | 125 mL Championship Barbecue Rub (page 51)

apple juice in a spray bottle

Ron's Rich, Deeply Satisfying Dipping Sauce
(page 60) or your favorite Kansas City–style sauce

Prepare your smoker for barbecuing, bringing the temperature up to 200–220°F/95–100°C. Cut along the gristly part of the ribs to separate each rack from the breast plate. Remove the shiny membrane on the inside of the ribs.

Coat the ribs evenly with mustard on both sides. Sprinkle lightly with garlic, then give the ribs a medium coating of rub, coating the convex (inner) side first and finishing with the convex side facing down (this prevents the rub from getting smudged).

Let the ribs sit for at least 15 minutes or until the rub starts to draw moisture out of the meat and looks shiny.

Place the ribs, with the convex side up (⌒), on the cooking grate or place the ribs on a rib rack. Cook for 5 to 7 hours, depending on the size of the ribs, spraying with apple juice at the 3-hour point and then again about every hour or so.

At the beginning of the last hour of cooking, paint the ribs with a light coating of barbecue sauce.

Half an hour before the end of the cooking time, test the ribs for doneness. If they pass the pull test (see Barbecue Secret, top right), give them one more coat of sauce, wrap them in foil and return them to the cooker for another half an hour or so.

Remove from the cooker and let the wrapped ribs rest for 20 to 45 minutes. Unwrap, cut into single ribs, and serve with your favorite accompaniments.

BARBECUE ⊱ SECRETS ⊰

To test ribs for doneness, use the pull test. Grab the outer two ribs with your thumbs and fore-fingers and gently pull them apart. If they are bonded tightly, the ribs are not yet done. If the meat pulls apart easily, the ribs are ready to take out of the cooker.

⊱ ⊰

Pork rib membrane is slippery and frustrating to remove unless you use this technique: separate a corner of the membrane from the rib cage with a sharp knife. Using a dry paper towel as a gripper, grab the loosened membrane and peel it off the ribs with steady pressure, reestablishing your grip as more membrane comes off. Once you have removed it, trim off any excess fat from the ribs, along with any remaining bits of membrane.

classic north CAROLINA barbecued pulled PORK sandwiches

Serves 18 to 24

The concept here is to cook a pork shoulder butt roast (sometimes called a Boston butt) for many hours in a smokey chamber until it is literally falling apart. One test competitors use for doneness is if the blade bone can actually be pulled out of the roast, the pork is ready to shred and serve. This is real barbecue the way we prepare it for competition, and the way it is eaten in the southeastern states. You can substitute any good rub you have on hand if you don't have time to make some from scratch, but fellow Butt Shredder Kathy Richardier's Butt Rub is the best! This recipe calls for two butts because if you're going to tend the smoker for such a long time you might as well fill it up. Pork butt freezes very well, so if you're not feeding a huge crowd just serve one of the butts, wrap the other in an extra layer of foil and freeze it for later use.

For Kathy's Butt Rub

1 Tbsp. | 15 mL kosher salt

2 Tbsp. | 25 mL sugar

2 Tbsp. | 25 mL brown sugar

2 Tbsp. | 25 mL cumin

2 Tbsp. | 25 mL chili powder (like Chimayo blend, New Mexico or Ancho)

2 Tbsp. | 25 mL ground black pepper

up to 1 Tbsp. | 15 mL cayenne

1/4 cup | 50 mL paprika

For the pulled pork sandwiches

2 pork shoulder butt roasts, about 6 to 9 lbs. | 2.7 to 3 kg each, bone in

1 cup | 250 mL prepared mustard

1 Tbsp. | 15 mL granulated garlic

apple juice/maple syrup/bourbon blend in a spray bottle (see Barbecue Secret on next page)

2 cups | 500 mL or more of Ron's Rich, Deeply Satisfying Dipping Sauce (page 60)

1 cup | 250 mL North Carolina–Style Vinegar Sauce (page 66)

2 dozen fresh, fluffy white buns

Tidewater Coleslaw (page 100)

Combine the rub ingredients and set aside.

Slather the butts with mustard, sprinkle with granulated garlic and then coat liberally with the rub. Let the rubbed butts sit for 1/2 hour until the meat's juices make the rub look wet and shiny.

Prepare your smoker for barbecuing, bringing the temperature up to 200–220°F/95–100°C. Line the drip pan of your smoker with a double layer of foil and fill it with apple juice. (If you want a more crispy crust on the butts, just line the drip pan and leave it dry.) Cook the butts for 1 1/2 hours per lb./500 g (about 8 to 10 hours), adding coals and chunks of hardwood as required. We use apple in competition.

About halfway through the cooking time, turn the butts and spray them with the apple juice mixture. Turn over and spray again at the 3/4 mark. Two hours before the butts are due to be ready, turn them over again and generously glaze with barbecue sauce and throw a couple of chunks of hardwood on the coals. An hour before they're due to be finished, turn and glaze the butts one more time and wrap them in a double coating of foil. One more hour in the smoker, then take them out. Let them rest for at least half an hour.

Take the butts out of the foil and place them in a large roasting pan or heavy duty roasting tray. Using two forks or your hands sheathed in rubber gloves, pull apart the pork, mixing the exterior crusty bits together with the tender, juicy white meat. Drizzle with the vinegar sauce and mix it into the shredded meat.

To serve, pile the shredded pork on the buns, drizzle with some more vinegar sauce and/or some of your favorite barbecue sauce, and top with the coleslaw for a big, juicy, crunchy, messy barbecue sandwich. Take one bite and you will know what real barbecue tastes like!

VARIATION

Covered grill method: You can barbecue pork butts on your covered charcoal or gas grill. Follow the recipe above exactly, but use indirect low heat (this is easier on a gas grill because to maintain low heat on a charcoal grill means you have to add coals every hour or two for a whole day). Use soaked wood chips or chunks wrapped in foil and poked with a fork to create a bit of smoke. It won't be as smokey, but it'll still be good! The one advantage of this technique is you can probably get by with a couple hours less cooking time.

cheater RIBS

Serves 4

True barbecue people don't like to even *think* of this technique, which goes against all the principles and values of barbecue culture. These ribs may not be smokey, and they may not be as flavorful as true barbecued ribs, but they're wonderfully tender, they taste great, and they don't take all day to cook.

2 racks side or baby back ribs, trimmed by your butcher

1 medium onion, peeled and halved

1 tsp. | 5 mL peppercorns

3 or 4 whole cloves

2 Tbsp. | 25 mL prepared mustard

1/2 tsp. | 2 mL granulated garlic

1/4 cup | 50 mL or so Championship Barbecue Rub (page 51)

1 cup | 250 mL barbecue sauce, the sweeter and tangier the better

Remove the membrane from the ribs if your butcher hasn't already done it for you. Fill a large pot with cold water and completely submerge the ribs in the water. Add the onion, peppercorns and cloves. Bring the water just to a boil. With a spoon or ladle, quickly skim off the soapy scum that forms on the top of the water and reduce the heat to low. Gently simmer the ribs for about 1$\frac{1}{4}$ hours, or until they just pass the pull test (see Barbecue Secrets on page 125). Take the ribs out of the water and cool them on a cooking sheet until they are easy to handle.

Prepare your grill for direct medium heat. Coat the ribs with mustard, sprinkle lightly with garlic and coat with the rub. Let sit until the rub starts to glisten, about 10 minutes. Grill the ribs for 3 or 4 minutes on each side, applying barbecue sauce with a basting brush as you turn them. Cook until the sauce is nicely caramelized and the ribs are lightly charred in a few places. Remove from the grill, let them rest for a few minutes, cut them into single ribs and serve with classic barbecue accompaniments like corn on the cob, slaw, beans, etc.

pork and apple KEBABS

Serves 8 as an appetizer or 4 to 6 as a main course

This is a great late-summer grilling dish. Use the tangiest, firmest, new crop apples you can find. Serve as an appetizer, or with grilled vegetables (see method page 74) and Dilled Smashed Potatoes (page 96) as a main course.

To marinate the pork

2 lbs. | 1 kg boneless pork loin

1 tsp. | 5 mL granulated onion

1 clove garlic, forced through a garlic press

1 Tbsp. | 15 mL fresh rosemary

1 tsp. | 5 mL dried rosemary

1/2 tsp. | 2 mL allspice

1/4 tsp. | 1 mL freshly grated nutmeg

pinch cayenne

pinch cloves

1/4 cup | 50 mL cider vinegar

For the kebabs

6 apples, peeled, cored and cut into bite-sized chunks

kosher salt and freshly ground black pepper to taste

extra virgin olive oil

Cut the pork into bite-sized chunks. Combine the marinade ingredients in a nonreactive bowl and add the pork, mixing thoroughly. Marinate for about 1 hour at room temperature or 2 or 3 hours in the fridge.

Prepare your grill for medium direct heat. Thread the pork chunks on 8 long metal skewers or 12 presoaked bamboo skewers, alternating with chunks of apple. Grill the kebabs for 3 to 4 minutes per side or until the pork is just done. Season with salt and pepper and drizzle with a little oil.

POULTRY

Chicken is so ubiquitous in modern North American cuisine that it has almost become invisible, part of a kind of culinary background noise that takes up space on fast food menus and makes for totally forgettable home cooking. We make it worse by insisting that chicken be cooked to extreme temperatures, creating dry, stringy, rubbery stuff that only barely qualifies as food.

In championship barbecue it's one of the hardest dishes to get just right. The skin can go rubbery in the moist chamber of the cooker, or it can be overcooked to the point where it becomes grainy and just tastes like smoke.

But when cooked properly on a grill, or barbecued to smokey perfection, chicken can transcend its boring modern life to transport us to a place where comfort food and dining adventure meet.

One more thing. It's worth the money to buy more full-flavored free-range organic chickens. I like the corn-fed ones that have more yellow skin and orange-toned flesh.

southwestern chicken CLUB sandwich

Serves 2 to 4

You may never go back to Subway after eating this juicy, tender chicken club sandwich, a great post-golf Saturday lunch. Serve with cold beer or a crisp, fruity white wine.

For the rub

1 Tbsp. | 15 mL kosher salt

1 Tbsp. | 15 mL granulated garlic

1 Tbsp. | 15 mL granulated onion

1 Tbsp. | 15 mL ground coriander seed

1 Tbsp. | 15 mL ground toasted cumin seed

1 tsp. | 5 mL cayenne

1 tsp. | 5 mL freshly ground black pepper

To make the sandwiches

4 large boneless skinless chicken breasts, fillet removed

extra virgin olive oil

4 soft white hoagie buns

softened butter

granulated garlic

1 lemon

kosher salt and freshly ground black pepper to taste

1 cup | 250 mL Chipotle and Roasted Garlic Aïoli (page 73)

1 bunch fresh arugula, washed and dried

2 large ripe tomatoes, thinly sliced

1 purple onion, peeled and thinly sliced

Combine the rub ingredients and set aside. Prepare your grill for medium direct heat.

Place the chicken breasts, one at a time, in a large resealable plastic bag (or between two sheets of plastic wrap) and pound with a mallet or champagne bottle (they're sturdier than regular wine bottles) until they are flattened to an even 1/2 inch / 1 cm thickness. Place the flattened breasts on a platter or cookie sheet and sprinkle each breast generously with the rub on both sides. Drizzle the breasts with olive oil to moisten the rub. Prepare the buns by slicing them in half, buttering them and sprinkling the buttered sides with garlic. When the grill is hot, place the breasts, oiled side down, on the cooking grate, close the grill and cook for no more than 1 or 2 minutes per side. After you have turned the breasts, put the buns on the grill, buttered side down. When the breasts are just barely done and the buns are nicely toasted, transfer to a clean plate. Drizzle the breasts with a little olive oil and a squeeze of lemon and season with salt and pepper.

Generously slather the toasted buns with the aïoli and make a bed of arugula on the bottom half of each bun. Place the chicken breasts on the arugula and top with the tomato and onion slices, again seasoning with a little salt and pepper. Close the sandwiches and slice in half.

mediterranean ROAST CHICKEN

Serves 4

This is a great way to roast chicken. Don't use too much hardwood or it will overpower the flavor of the herbed rub. Serve with Dilled Smashed Potatoes (page 96) and Roasted Vegetables or Dilled Lemony Rice (page 94).

1 5-lb. | 2.2-kg chicken

kosher salt to taste

1 Tbsp. | 15 mL Dijon mustard

2 Tbsp. | 25 mL Mediterranean Dried Herb Rub (page 54)

1 Tbsp. | 15 mL coarsely chopped fresh rosemary

1 tsp. | 5 mL freshly ground black pepper

1 tsp. | 5 mL granulated garlic

1 tsp. | 5 mL granulated onion

1/2 tsp. | 2 mL cayenne

1/2 cup | 125 mL extra virgin olive oil

juice of 1/2 lemon

Prepare your grill for indirect medium heat, with a drip pan underneath the unheated portion of the grill to catch the drippings. Rinse the chicken in cold water and pat dry with paper towels. Generously season with salt and coat with mustard. Combine the herbed rub, rosemary, pepper, garlic, onion and cayenne in a small bowl. Coat the chicken with the mixture, patting it on with your hands to ensure it sticks. Drizzle the rubbed chicken with 1 Tbsp./15 mL of the olive oil. Place the chicken, breast side up, on the unheated side of the cooking grate.

In a small bowl, combine the rest of the oil with the lemon juice.

Cook the chicken, using a small amount of fruitwood as a flavoring agent, for about an hour, basting every 20 minutes or so with the oil/lemon juice mixture, until the internal temperature at the thickest part of the thigh reaches 160°F/71°C. Remove from the grill, tent with foil and let rest for 10 to 15 minutes. Carve and serve immediately.

BIG DADDY'S barbecued Thai chicken thighs

Serves 4

Ian "Big Daddy" Baird is a sometime Butt Shredder who has traveled in Asia. He tells me that one of the best pieces of meat he's ever eaten was a whole chicken thigh and drumstick he purchased from a street vendor out the window of a train as he waited to cross the Thai/Malaysian border. He tried numerous times to re-create it himself, but it wasn't until he married this recipe with real barbeque technique that he came close. Serve with Coconut Johnnycakes (page 108) and cold beer.

For the chicken

10 to 12 chicken thighs, bone in, skin on

6 Tbsp. | 90 mL fresh lime juice
(1 large lime)

1/4 cup | 50 mL fresh orange juice
(1 medium orange)

1/4 cup | 50 mL Thai fish sauce

1/4 cup | 50 mL peanut or canola oil

1/4 cup | 50 mL raw sugar or
lightly packed brown sugar

1 Tbsp. | 15 mL Asian chili sauce

2 Tbsp. | 25 mL finely minced ginger

5 to 10 cloves garlic, finely minced

1/4 cup | 50 mL minced fresh basil

1/4 cup | 50 mL green onions

1/4 cup | 50 mL cilantro

For the basting mixture

1/2 cup | 125 mL peanut oil

juice of 1 lime

Trim the chicken thighs of excess fat. Mix all the remaining ingredients together and put them in a resealable plastic bag. Place the chicken in the bag, remove the air, and seal. Marinate at least 2 and up to a maximum of 8 hours in the fridge.

Prepare your smoker for barbecuing, bringing the temperature up to 200–220°F/95–100°C. Make the basting mixture by combining the oil and lime juice in a bowl.

Discard the marinade and place the chicken in the smoker for 2 1/2 hours, turning and basting every hour. If you wish give the skin side a quick 30 seconds on a hot grill to really crisp the skin.

tikka-style chicken kebabs

Serves 4

My friend Jagreet's mom, a great East Indian home cook, shared her chicken marinade recipe with me, and I'm sharing it with you. Serve these kebabs on a bed of steamed basmati rice with some of your favorite chutney and Curried Vegetables (page 92) on the side.

To marinate the chicken

1 cup | 250 mL plain yoghurt

3 Tbsp. | 45 mL neutral-flavored oil, such as canola or peanut

3 Tbsp. | 45 mL minced ginger

3 Tbsp. | 45 mL minced garlic

1 tsp. | 5 mL kosher salt

2 Tbsp. | 25 mL lime juice

1 Tbsp. | 15 mL tandoori paste

1 Tbsp. | 15 mL garam masala spice

1 large purple onion, peeled and cut into chunks

4 large boneless, skinless chicken breasts, cut into bite-sized chunks

1 lime

To finish the kebabs

olive or canola oil

kosher salt to taste

1 lime

In a nonreactive bowl combine the yoghurt, oil, ginger, garlic, salt, lime juice, tandoori paste and masala spice and mix well. Add the onion chunks and chicken, cover with plastic wrap and marinate overnight in the refrigerator.

Prepare your grill for medium direct heat. Thread the chicken chunks and onion pieces onto 8 presoaked bamboo skewers. Grill the kebabs for 4 to 6 minutes, turning 2 or 3 times. (Don't overcook or the chicken will have a mealy texture!) Remove from the grill, drizzle with a little oil, season with salt to taste, squeeze some fresh lime juice over each skewer and serve immediately.

dilled yoghurt chicken kebabs

Serves 12 as an appetizer or 4 to 6 as a main course

Yoghurt and dill do something wonderful to chicken. Using boneless, skinless chicken thighs gives these kebabs added richness. Serve as an appetizer or as a main course with Field Greens with Walnut Oil and Toasted Pumpkin Seeds (page 102) and Dilled Lemony Rice (page 94).

2 lbs. | 1 kg boneless, skinless chicken thighs,
cut into bite-sized chunks

1 cup | 250 mL plain full-fat yoghurt

1/2 cup | 125 mL fresh chopped dill

1/2 tsp. | 2 mL dried dill weed

1 Tbsp. | 15 mL granulated onion

2 cloves garlic, forced through a garlic press

juice of 1/2 lemon

pinch cayenne

grinding of black pepper

2 medium sweet white onions, quartered and separated into bite-sized
chunks (or use a cut-up fennel bulb, or a combination of the two)

1 lemon cut into wedges

kosher salt and freshly ground black pepper to taste

olive oil for drizzling

Combine the chicken chunks with the yoghurt, dill, onion, garlic, lemon juice, cayenne and pepper in a nonreactive container and refrigerate for at least 2 hours or as long as overnight.

Thread the chicken pieces on 8 metal skewers or 12 pre-soaked bamboo skewers, alternating with the onion or fennel chunks. Prepare your grill for direct medium heat. Place the kebabs on the grate and cook for 3 to 5 minutes per side or until just done. Take the kebabs off the grill, season with salt and pepper, drizzle with some olive oil and serve immediately. Garnish with lemon wedges.

Tuscan grilled game hens

Serves 2 as a single course or 4 as part of a multi-course meal

This is a delicious way to enjoy Cornish game hens. I have adapted this recipe from my Italophile brother, Allan. Serve these with your favorite risotto, polenta or pasta with a creamy sauce and some grilled vegetables. If time allows, season the hens and refrigerate for several hours before cooking.

2 Cornish game hens

1/4 medium onion

3 large cloves garlic

1/4 cup | 50 mL tightly packed fresh basil leaves

1/2 tsp. | 2 mL dried basil

1/4 tsp. | 1 mL dried oregano

1/4 tsp. | 1 mL dried marjoram

4 slices (1½ to 2 oz. | 40 to 50 g) pancetta, chopped

5 Tbsp. | 75 mL high-quality balsamic vinegar

1 Tbsp. | 15 mL extra virgin olive oil

kosher salt and freshly ground black pepper to taste

1/2 to 1 cup | 125 to 250 mL dry white wine

1/2 cup | 125 mL olive oil

fresh parsley or thyme sprigs, for garnish

Wash the hens and pat dry with paper towels. In a food processor or by hand, mince the onion, garlic, fresh and dried herbs, and pancetta. Blend 2 tsp. / 10 mL of the vinegar and the 1 Tbsp. / 15 mL oil. Season with salt and pepper.

Cut the hens' backbones and open them out flat, skin side up. With your palm, firmly press down the breast area to flatten. Stuff most of the herb mixture under the skin of the thigh, leg and breast areas. Rub the rest all over the hens.

Prepare your grill for medium indirect cooking with a pan underneath the cooking grate to catch the drippings. Combine the wine and the 1/2 cup / 125 mL oil. When your grill is up to temperature, place the birds skin side up on the grate above the drip pan. Grill for 20 minutes, baste with the wine mixture, and turn. Cook for another 20 minutes, basting and turning every 5 minutes or so, until the internal temperature at the base of the thigh is 160°F/71°C. If the hens are not golden brown by this time, crisp them, skin side down, over direct heat for a few minutes, watching out for flare-ups, before taking them off the grill.

Let the hens rest for 5 minutes tented with foil. Drizzle with oil, season with salt and pepper and garnish with fresh parsley or thyme sprigs before serving.

Kate's **TASTY ASIAN** chicken thighs

Serves 4 to 6

These tangy, flavorful chicken thighs, based on a recipe by Anya Von Bremzen and Jon Welchman in their *Terrific Pacific Cookbook*, go well with Asian Noodle Salad with Sesame Mayonnaise (page 105). This recipe calls for grilling, but you can also barbecue the chicken in a smoker for a truly unforgettable dish and then finish it by crisping the skin on a hot grill.

12 chicken thighs ($3^1/2$ lbs. | 1.75 kg), bone in, skin on

2 tsp. | 10 mL ground coriander

1 tsp. | 5 mL freshly ground black pepper

1 tsp. | 5 mL kosher salt

$1^1/2$ Tbsp. | 20 mL tamarind pulp (Thai is best)

1/3 cup | 75 mL chicken stock or tinned broth, boiling

6 Asian dried red chiles (2 to 3 inches | 5 to 8 cm)

4 large cloves garlic, chopped

3 Tbsp. | 45 mL chopped shallots

2 tsp. | 10 mL chopped fresh ginger

1 Tbsp. | 15 mL chopped fresh lemon grass or
2 tsp. | 10 mL grated lime zest

$1^1/2$ Tbsp. | 22 mL vegetable oil

3 Tbsp. | 45 mL dark soy sauce

3 Tbsp. | 45 mL packed light brown sugar

$1^1/2$ Tbsp. | 20 mL rice vinegar

$1^1/2$ Tbsp. | 20 mL ketchup

1/2 cup | 125 mL finely chopped fresh basil

Rinse the chicken pieces well and pat dry with paper towels. Prick the skin all over with the tines of a fork. In a small bowl, combine the coriander, pepper and salt and rub into the chicken pieces. Set aside.

Add the tamarind pulp to the boiling stock, remove from the heat, and soak for 15 minutes. Stir and mash it with a fork to help it dissolve. Strain through a fine strainer into a bowl, pressing on the solids with the back of a wooden spoon to extract all the liquid. Set aside.

Stem the chiles and shake out and discard the seeds. Using scissors, cut the chiles into 1/4-inch/5-mm pieces. Soak in warm water to cover for 10 minutes. Drain well.

Combine the chiles, tamarind liquid, garlic, shallots, ginger, lemon grass or lime zest, oil, soy sauce, sugar, vinegar, ketchup, and basil in a food processor and process to a purée. Arrange the chicken in a large shallow dish and pour the marinade over it. Cover and refrigerate for at least 2 hours, but preferably overnight.

Remove the chicken pieces from the marinade and pour the marinade into a saucepan. Heat to a boil and let simmer for 10 minutes. Taste and adjust the seasonings. Remove from the heat and transfer to a bowl.

Prepare your grill for indirect medium heat, with a pan underneath the unheated side of the grill to catch the drippings. Place the chicken on the grill and cook for 20 to 25 minutes or until the internal temperature reaches 160°F/71°C, basting every 5 minutes with the marinade. At the last minute, move the chicken thighs to the hot side of the grill and toss them about to crisp the skins, taking care not to burn them. Place the chicken on a serving dish, spoon over the remaining basting sauce and serve immediately.

smoked **chicken** FAJITAS

Serves 4

When you are doing traditional barbecue and have some extra capacity in your cooker, it's never a bad idea to smoke a few chickens for later using the classic "mustard and rub" method. I like to always have one or two on hand in the freezer. Smoked chicken meat makes great chicken salad and is a good addition to a pasta sauce, or you can reheat it on your grill, slice it up and toss it into a green salad. One of the greatest uses for leftover smoked chicken is this fajita recipe.

For the chicken

1 5-lb. | 2.2-kg whole chicken

2 Tbsp. | 25 mL mustard

1 tsp. | 5 mL granulated garlic

2 Tbsp. | 25 mL Championship Barbecue Rub (page 51)

1/2 tsp. | 2 mL powdered ginger

1/2 tsp. | 2 mL five-spice powder

1/2 tsp. | 2 mL mustard powder

1/4 cup | 50 mL melted butter

juice of 1 lemon

For the fajitas

1 Tbsp. | 15 mL olive or vegetable oil

1 medium onion, halved and sliced into 1/2-inch | 1-cm strips

1 clove garlic, finely chopped

1/2 lb. | 250 g button mushrooms, thinly sliced

1 red bell pepper, sliced into 1/2-inch | 1-cm strips

1 Tbsp. | 15 mL ground ancho chiles or your favorite chili powder

1 tsp. | 5 mL cumin

1 tsp. | 5 mL ground coriander

1/4 tsp. | 1 mL ground cinnamon

pinch ground cloves

pinch cayenne

1/2 cup | 125 mL dry white wine

1 cup | 250 mL chicken or vegetable stock

kosher salt and freshly ground black pepper to taste

12 warmed flour tortillas

cilantro, for garnish

Prepare your smoker for barbecuing, bringing the temperature up to 200–220°F/95–100°C. Halve the chicken lengthwise, removing the backbone with kitchen shears. Spread the mustard on both sides of the chicken and lightly sprinkle with granulated garlic. Combine the rub with the ginger, five-spice and mustard. Coat the chicken with the mixture and let stand for 10 or 20 minutes until the rub starts to glisten. Place skin side up on the cooking grate and smoke for 3 to 3½ hours or until the internal temperature is 160°F/71°C, using fruitwood as the flavoring agent. Combine the butter and lemon juice and baste the chicken every hour or so.

At this point you can just eat the chicken. If you like a crispy skin, place the smoked chicken skin side down on a hot grill (or under a broiler) for a few minutes at the end of cooking, taking care to avoid flare-ups. Let it rest for 15 minutes before serving, or cool and store until you need it. Refrigerates for a week or freezes well for a few months.

To make the fajitas, tear the chicken off the bones and cut the meat into ½-inch/1-cm strips or bite-sized chunks. Heat the oil in a cast iron skillet or nonstick frying pan over medium-high heat. Toss in the onion and garlic and sauté until transparent. Add the mushrooms and bell pepper and sauté until tender. Add the chicken pieces and toss until heated through. Sprinkle in the chili powder, cumin, coriander, cinnamon, cloves and cayenne and toss until the spices are blended thoroughly into the mixture. Add the wine and reduce until the liquid disappears. Add the stock and reduce until the liquid is barely gone, the mixture is fragrant, shiny and moist and the chicken is tender and slightly shredded. Adjust the seasoning with salt and pepper. Spoon into warmed flour tortillas, sprinkle with a little cilantro and enjoy.

The Wings Variations

Chicken wings are so easy to grill or barbecue. To trim, just cut the wing tips off and discard. I like to leave the wing/drummettes together, but you can separate them if you like. Flavor the wings with your favorite rub or marinade. On the grill, cook for 8 to 12 minutes using medium-to-high direct heat, turning regularly, until they are almost charred, basting with your favorite barbecue sauce for the last few minutes of cooking. To barbecue, prepare your smoker for barbecuing, bringing the temperature up to 200–220°F/95–100°C. Cook the wings for about an hour with hickory, mesquite or fruitwood as flavoring agents and then crisp them up on a grill if you like. They're great just with mustard and Championship Barbecue Rub (page 51), but try these variations.

Fiery Southwestern Wings

Make a simple rub with 1 part powdered chipotles, 1 part ancho chile powder and 1 part garlic salt. Grill till crispy, finish with a drizzling of olive oil, a pinch of kosher salt and a squeeze of lemon.

Teriyaki Wings

Marinate wings in teriyaki sauce for 2 hours. Grill till crispy, basting with more sauce. Finish with extra sauce and a sprinkle of toasted sesame seeds.

Buffalo–Style Grilled Wings

Melt 1/4 cup/50 ml of butter and add 1/2 cup/125 mL of Louisiana–style hot sauce (Franks, Tabasco, etc.). Salt and pepper the wings and grill till crispy. Take the wings off the grill and immediately toss them in the butter/hot sauce mixture. Serve with blue cheese dressing and celery sticks.

Lemon Dijon Rosemary Wings

Season the wings with salt and pepper and coat with Dijon mustard. Sprinkle with dried rosemary and a very light dusting of cayenne. Grill until crispy, season with a little more salt and pepper, and squeeze a lemon over them just before serving.

Cumin Seed Wings

Season the wings, coat with mustard, sprinkle with Championship Barbecue Rub (page 51) and coat lightly with cumin seeds. Grill till crispy, drizzle with olive oil and season with salt and pepper.

BEEF

What can one say of beef, the King of Meats? So many variations, so much flavor, and so easy to cook. Salt and pepper and a hot fire are all you really need for a profound beef experience. This section of the book is my humble tribute to what, in the end, is my all-around favorite food.

cowboy STEAKS

Serves 4

This is pretty close to my favorite steak. The earthiness of the cumin seeds, the sharpness of the cracked pepper, the sweetness of the onion and garlic granules, and the smokey, tart bite of the ground chipotles create an explosion of flavor. Serve whole steaks with beans, a slab of cornbread and some coleslaw. Alternative serving suggestion: slice up the steaks and serve them fajita–style with salsa, guacamole and shredded Jack cheese with some warm flour tortillas.

4 big rib-eye steaks, bone in, about 1¹/₂ inches | 4 cm thick

kosher salt (or another fancy coarse salt like Malden or
fleur de sel) to taste

1/2 cup | 125 mL black peppercorns

1 Tbsp. | 15 mL granulated onion

1 Tbsp. | 15 mL granulated garlic

1 tsp. | 5 mL ground chipotle chiles
(if you can't find chipotles, use cayenne)

1 Tbsp. | 15 mL toasted cumin seeds

extra virgin olive oil

Place the steaks in a dish or on a large cutting board and let them come to room temperature (about an hour). Use a spice mill or a mortar and pestle to give the peppercorns a coarse grinding, or put them in a thick paper or plastic bag and pound them with a hammer or rolling pin until they reach the desired consistency. They shouldn't be powdery, but more like coarse sand. Generously season the steaks with the salt and pepper. Combine the granulated onion and garlic, ground chipotles and cumin seeds in a bowl. Coat the steaks on one side with the mixture, patting it on so it sticks nicely. Drizzle the rubbed steaks with a light coating of olive oil, turn them over and repeat the seasoning, rub, and oil drizzle.

Prepare your grill for medium direct heat and cook the steaks for about 4 to 6 minutes per side for medium-rare. If using a charcoal grill, toss a couple of chunks of mesquite (or a handful of chips) onto the coals just prior to grilling. With a gas grill, use a foil pack of pre-soaked chips with holes punched into it with a fork.

Be sure not to overcook the steaks! Remember, they will continue to cook after they are taken off the heat. Remove them from the grill and let them rest for 4 or 5 minutes before serving.

beautiful **BRONTO** beef ribs

Serves 4 to 6

These are the ribs that tipped over Fred Flintstone's car. You can use the rub on anything, but it goes exceptionally well with this dish.

1 Tbsp. | 15 mL black peppercorns

1 Tbsp. | 15 mL dried mushrooms
(porcini, morels or chanterelles work well)

1 tsp. | 5mL cumin seeds

1 Tbsp. | 15 mL ground ancho chile

1/2 tsp. | 2 mL ground chipotles or cayenne

2 racks beef prime ribs, 6 to 8 bones per rack

kosher salt

olive oil

Using a spice mill or electric coffee grinder, grind the pepper, dried mushrooms and cumin seeds until they have the consistency of coarse sand. Combine with the ground ancho and chipotle chiles. Season the ribs with a generous coating of salt and then give them a light drizzle of oil. Coat liberally with the rub. Let the ribs sit for up to 1/2 hour, or until the rub starts to glisten.

Prepare the grill for medium indirect cooking with a pan to catch the drippings. Grill the ribs for 1 hour, turning every 15 minutes or so and basting with olive oil, until the internal temperature in the thickest part of the ribs reaches 140°F/60°C. For the last 10 minutes of cooking time, put the ribs over direct heat to char and crisp them up. You can finish these up with your favorite barbecue sauce but I prefer them just like this. Serve with classic barbecue accompaniments.

Alternative cooking method: for a whole other layer of flavor, smoke these ribs for 4 to 5 hours, using oak or mesquite as a flavoring agent, and finish them on the grill.

Cedar-Planked Salmon with Bourbon-Maple Glaze
page 178

Dilled and Grilled Halibut Steaks with Field Greens with Walnut Oil and Toasted Pumpkin Seeds
pages 164 and 102

The Ultimate Triple-Chocolate Brownies
page 180

Bourbon and Honey Planked Peaches

page 195

VINCE'S **herbed** veal ribs

Serves 4

Vince Gogolek is a fellow Butt Shredder who has perfected this recipe for veal ribs. They are not usually available in supermarkets, but if you can find them at a butcher shop, they make a delicious alternative to pork or beef ribs. They are also relatively inexpensive (for veal, anyway). This recipe uses a fresh herb rub, which acts like a marinade, getting the herb flavor deep into the meat. Serve with grilled vegetables and Dilled Smashed Potatoes (page 96).

1 rack veal ribs (about 2 to 3 lbs. | 1 to 1.5 kg)

1/4 cup | 50 mL fresh rosemary, finely chopped

1/4 cup | 50 mL fresh parsley leaves, finely chopped

2 Tbsp. | 25 mL fresh oregano leaves, finely chopped

2 fresh basil leaves, finely chopped

4 fresh sage leaves, finely chopped

2 cloves garlic, finely minced

1/2 cup | 125 mL olive oil

2 Tbsp. | 25 mL kosher salt

2 Tbsp. | 25 mL coarsely ground black pepper

Remove the shiny membrane from the back of the ribs. Combine all the remaining ingredients and apply the herb rub to the ribs, ensuring it gets into all the crevices so it can permeate the meat like a marinade. Refrigerate overnight.

Prepare your grill for medium direct heat. Grill for an hour using direct medium heat to brown the ribs and get grill marks, then move to indirect heat for another hour after browning. Or, for extra flavor, smoke the ribs for 5 hours using fruitwood as the flavoring agent.

EASIEST, tastiest steak

Serves 4

I have been grilling steaks bathed in this marinade for over 20 years and I have not found a way to improve on it. It's so easy and adds so much flavor that every backyard cook should have it in his or her repertoire. These go well with just about any side. I like them with roasted baby potatoes and grilled asparagus. The marinade is also great with pork chops, as well as rich, meaty fish like salmon, halibut, tuna and swordfish.

1 cup | 250 mL dark soy sauce

1 tsp. | 5 mL toasted sesame oil

2 cloves garlic, finely minced

1 Tbsp. | 15 mL finely chopped or grated fresh ginger

freshly ground black pepper to taste

juice of 1/2 a lemon or 1/4 cup | 50 mL Chinese rice cooking wine

1 Tbsp. | 15 mL tapioca starch (cornstarch will also do)

4 well-marbled rib steaks, about 1$\frac{1}{2}$ inches | 4 cm thick

Mix the soy sauce, sesame oil, garlic, ginger, black pepper, lemon juice or cooking wine and tapioca starch in a nonreactive baking dish. Add the meat, turn to coat, and marinate 10 minutes to $\frac{1}{2}$ hour, turning once or twice. Do not marinate overnight, as this is a fairly salty marinade.

Prepare your grill for medium direct heat. Place the steaks on the grill and cook for about 4 minutes. Turn the steaks, spoon a little more marinade on the top, and then cook for another 4 minutes for medium-rare. Let them rest about 4 minutes and serve.

beef KEBABS

Serves 4 as a main course, 8 as an appetizer

Most beef kebab recipes, including this one, call for using leaner cuts like sirloin. These work well, but they are quite chewy and can turn to rubber if overcooked. For truly decadent kebabs, try well-marbled rib roast or tender chunks of fillet. Whatever meat you choose, just remember to cook it gently and don't overdo it!

To marinate the meat

2 Tbsp. | 25 mL dried mushrooms (any kind will do, but some can be expensive)

1 Tbsp. | 15 mL ground ancho chile

1 tsp. | 5 mL ground cumin

1 tsp. | 5 mL ground cinnamon

1 tsp. | 5 mL coarsely ground black pepper

1 chipotle in adobo sauce, seeds removed and finely chopped

1 tsp. | 5 mL adobo sauce

1 Tbsp. | 15 mL liquid honey

1/2 cup | 125 mL neutral-flavored vegetable oil like canola or corn oil

2 lbs. | 1 kg top sirloin

To make the kebabs

2 Tbsp. | 25 mL vegetable oil

juice of 1 lime

2 red bell peppers, cut into chunks

2 yellow bell peppers, cut into chunks

1 medium purple onion, cut into quarters and separated into pieces

24 small button mushrooms (or 12 big ones cut in half)

kosher salt and freshly ground black pepper to taste

Grind the mushrooms to a powder in a spice mill or coffee grinder. In a nonreactive bowl, thoroughly mix the mushrooms, chile, cumin, cinnamon, pepper, chipotle, adobo sauce, honey and oil. Cut the beef into bite-size cubes and add to the marinade, tossing well to coat. Marinate for at least 2 hours and as long as overnight.

Make a basting liquid by combining the oil and lime juice. Prepare your grill for medium direct heat. Thread the beef cubes on 8 long metal skewers or 12 presoaked bamboo skewers, alternating with chunks of bell pepper, onion and mushroom. Grill 3 to 4 minutes per side, basting with the oil/lime juice mixture, until the beef is just done. Remove from the grill, season with salt and pepper and serve.

grill-roasted TRI-TIP

Serves 6 to 8

Tri-tip is the bottom half of a sirloin roast. It looks like a mini brisket but it's more tender and does not need long cooking because it doesn't have as much connective tissue. Tri-tip is a popular category in the latest trend on the barbecue circuit, the "Light Barbecue," which means the events are constructed so the competitors don't have to stay up all night. This recipe draws on classic Mediterranean flavors. It is great fresh off the grill or smoker, and just as good cold the next day, thinly sliced with some coarse salt and Dijon mustard. For perfect tri-tip, be sure not to overcook it—and let the roast rest for half an hour tented in foil so it retains its copious and delicious juices. I like to drizzle the slices with a little extra olive oil, sprinkle some salt on them and serve them with Dilled Smashed Potatoes (page 96) and roasted vegetables.

1 3-lb. | 1.5-kg well-marbled tri-tip (bottom sirloin) roast

kosher salt to taste

3 cloves garlic, peeled and coarsely chopped

2 large shallots

1/2 tsp. | 2 mL crushed red chiles

1 Tbsp. | 15 mL fresh rosemary

1 tsp. | 5 mL dried oregano

1 Tbsp. | 15 mL coarsely ground black pepper

1/4 cup | 50 mL extra virgin olive oil

Let the roast sit out of the fridge for half an hour to an hour to bring it up to room temperature. Prepare the grill for medium indirect cooking with a pan underneath the grate to catch the drippings.

Place the remaining ingredients in a food processor and whiz until blended but not puréed. Coat the roast in the paste, reserving a couple of Tbsp./25 mL for basting, and let the roast sit until the grill is ready.

Grill the roast for 1 hour on the unheated side of the grill, using hickory wood as a flavoring agent. Turn once or twice and baste with the reserved paste. When the roast is nearly done (it starts to feel springy to the touch, or the temperature at the thickest part reaches about 130°F/54°C for medium rare), move it to the hot side of the grill, turn up the heat to high, and sear it on both sides for a few minutes to crisp up the crust. Remove the roast from the grill, tent it in foil and let it rest for at least half an hour.

Slice across the grain as thinly as you can and serve with your favorite accompaniments.

Don't poke
≻ that meat! ≺

When you poke a meat thermometer into a piece of meat and take it out, it creates a little hole that allows all the precious juices to flow out! If you are not used to judging doneness by feel, try to use an ovenproof meat thermometer that you can keep in the roast for the duration of the cooking time. Otherwise, if you absolutely have to poke a hole in the roast, plug it immediately after with a wedge of wood or a broken-off piece of chopstick. And don't accidentally leave a quick-read thermometer in the roast—you'll get a special molten plastic sauce.

the king of barbecue: BEEF BRISKET

Serves 10 to 16 depending on size of brisket and guest appetites

This sinewy, fatty cut of beef may not be something you see often on the supermarket shelves, but it is one of the most flavorful meats and it is the classic barbecue of Texas. The bigger the brisket, the juicer the end product. Smaller cuts can end up dry. Cooking a brisket requires a long-term commitment. Plan to do this on a day when you can stay around the house doing yard work or watching sports on TV. The process I have described here is as close as possible to what we do in competition. The end result is succulent, fork-tender slices of meat that need no accompaniment, but if you insist, serve with a little dipping sauce, some coleslaw, beans and pickled onions. The charred, fatty crust of the brisket can be cut off and roughly chopped to make "burnt ends" which are superb in a bun or thrown into some baked beans to give them an extra jolt of smokey, fatty flavor.

1 whole brisket, 10 to 14 pounds | 4.5 to 6 kg, with a nice white fat cap

3 qts. | 3 L apple juice

1 cup | 250 mL prepared mustard

1 Tbsp. | 15 mL granulated garlic

1 1/2 cups | 375 mL Championship Barbecue Rub (page 51) or Texas–Style Rub (page 52)

2 cups | 500 mL apple juice mixed with bourbon and maple syrup in a spray bottle (page 28)

2 cups | 500 mL Ron's Rich, Deeply Satisfying Dipping Sauce (page 60)

For large cuts like pork butts and briskets the rule of thumb is to cook them 1 1/2 hours per lb. / 500 g. That means a 10-lb. / 4.5-kg brisket will take 15 hours to cook, so you really need to start cooking it the night before. Your timing doesn't have to be exact, so you shouldn't have to get up at 3 in the morning to put on the roast. (I usually put a big brisket on just before going to bed, at about midnight). Sealed in foil and wrapped in a blanket (or in a 160°F/70°C oven), a cooked brisket can sit for a few hours before you serve.

Take your thawed brisket out of the fridge and let it sit for an hour or two so it starts to come up to room temperature. Prepare your smoker for barbecuing, bringing the temperature to 200–220°F/95–100°C. Make sure you line your water pan with a double layer of extra-wide foil and fill the pan with apple juice. Use as much charcoal or hardwood as your smoker or pit will hold. A good water smoker will hold close to 15 lbs./7 kg of charcoal, which will burn for almost 24 hours. (You should know your smoker before you attempt to cook a brisket.)

There should be a nice fat cap on the brisket. Trim excess fat off with a sharp knife so you're left with a layer about 1/8 to 1/4 inch/3 to 5 mm thick.

Coat the brisket with regular ballpark mustard. Sprinkle both sides with a light coating of granulated garlic. Coat both sides of the brisket with a heavy sprinkling of barbecue rub so that it is evenly coated.

Let the brisket rest for about half an hour until the rub starts to get moist and tacky—the salt in the rub pulls some of the juices out of the roast, and this helps to make a nice crust. Put the brisket, fat side up, into your smoker and place some hickory or mesquite chunks on top of the coals. Cook for 1 1/2 hours per lb./500 g.

The internal temperature of the brisket should rise very gradually throughout the cooking time, reaching a final temperature of about 180°F/82°C. If you are going to use a meat thermometer, keep it in the roast—don't use one that you poke into the meat every time you use it, because it will cause the juices to run out. Halfway through the cooking time (first thing in the morning), turn the brisket, spraying it on both sides with the apple juice/bourbon mixture. At this point be sure to add some more hardwood chunks and top up the water pan with hot water. Also, make sure you have plenty of coals left, and replenish if you're running low.

Three-quarters of the way through the cooking time, turn and spray again. About two hours before you take off the brisket, turn it and give it a good coating of barbecue sauce on both sides. Cook the sauce-coated brisket for about another half hour, just enough so that the sauce starts to set. Give the brisket one more coating of glaze, take it off the cooking grate and wrap it in a double layer of foil (the extra-wide works best). Put the wrapped brisket back to cook for 1 more hour.

Remove the brisket and let it rest for at least an hour. In competition, our briskets often rest for as many as 3 or 4 hours.

Take the brisket out of the foil and slice it, perpendicular to the grain, in about 1/8- to 1/4-inch slices. Serve just like that, on a plate, with a little BBQ sauce on the side for dipping.

Crazy Texas Punch
Serves 12

This festive, kitschy punch from my friend Amy may sound crazy, but it's a crowd-pleaser!

1 small box Jell-O
(I prefer strawberry or cherry, but any will do)

2 cups | 500 mL hot water

2 cups | 500 mL sugar

2 cups | 500 mL cold water

1 2-quart | 2 L can pineapple juice

2 2-quart | 2 L bottles ginger ale

13 oz. vodka or white rum

Combine the Jell-O, hot water and sugar and stir until completely dissolved. Add the cold water and pineapple juice. Pour into a 1-gallon/4-L milk carton that has been well rinsed and freeze overnight. Let thaw 2 to 4 hours (Amy says it only takes 1 hour in Texas). Remove the milk carton and put the semi-frozen brick in a large punch bowl. Add 1 of the bottles of ginger ale and the vodka or rum before serving. People like it so much you will need the extra bottle of ginger ale to pour in at the end.

steak, ITALIAN–STYLE

Serves 4

How to Tell When A ❧ Steak is Done ❧

Most barbecue cooks use meat thermometers to carefully monitor the internal temperature of big cuts of meat, but for most purposes you can easily tell whether a steak or chicken breast is done simply by applying pressure to it with your forefinger. If the meat does not spring back, it's still pretty raw. If it has a soft springiness it's medium rare and ready to take off the grill. If you press it and it feels firm and stiff, it's overdone. Here's a great way to learn these hand readings: Hold your left hand in front of your chest, palm side down. Touch the meaty area between your thumb and forefinger. That's what rare meat feels like. Now, extend your fingers so they are evenly spread out in the universal "stop right there" sign. Press the same place and you'll find out what medium rare meat should feel like. Now make a fist and press again. That's well done, and if your meat feels like this you should make use of the fist you just made and punch yourself in the forehead.

The Ruby Lake Restaurant on the Sunshine Coast of British Columbia serves great Italian food in a rustic resort setting. On some days the restaurant owners put a fresh trout on a stump near the restaurant patio and a local bald eagle makes a show of swooping down and grabbing the fish in its talons. I had a juicy T-bone there once that showed me that sometimes the simplest treatments are the best ones when you're grilling a steak.

4 well-marbled T-bone steaks, at least 1 inch | 2.5 cm thick

kosher or Malden salt and coarsely ground black pepper to taste

dried Greek oregano

best-quality extra virgin olive oil

lemon wedges

1 bunch fresh arugula, washed and dried

Bring the steaks to room temperature by leaving them out of the fridge for an hour. Season them generously on both sides with the salt and pepper. Drizzle lightly with olive oil. Prepare your grill for direct medium heat. Grill 4 to 6 minutes per side or until it's done how you like it (I recommend taking it off the heat when the steak just slightly springs back when poked, which is an internal temperature of about 135°F/57°C.) Remove from the grill and let the steaks rest for 4 or 5 minutes. Make a little bed of arugula on each plate and put the steaks on top. Crumble a little oregano on each steak, drizzle with olive oil and season with a little more salt and freshly ground pepper. Garnish with lemon wedges. The juice and oil from the steak and the squeeze of lemon will create a fabulous natural dressing for the slightly bitter arugula.

the PERFECT pan-fried steak

Serves 1

This is not grilling, nor is it barbecue, but it fits with the spirit of this book. A cast iron skillet gives steak a crust you just can't get on a grill. This is the kind of steak I like to cook for myself when I'm home alone. Sometimes I just eat it standing at the stove, carving it up right in the pan. It needs no accompaniment except your favorite beverage. Wine, beer and martinis work nicely. If you really want to get fancy, place the steak on a bed of fresh bitter greens or next to a pile of Dilled Smashed Potatoes (page 96). For a classic American side, serve with a wedge of iceberg lettuce with some of your favorite blue cheese dressing poured over the top.

1 2-inch-thick | 5-cm well-marbled rib steak or T-bone

1 clove garlic

1 tsp. | 5 mL kosher salt

2 Tbsp. | 25 mL coarsely ground or cracked black peppercorns

3 Tbsp. | 45 mL butter, at room temperature

2 Tbsp. | 25 mL extra virgin olive oil

1 4-inch | 10-cm sprig of rosemary

1/2 cup | 125 mL red wine

Preheat the oven to 425°F/220°C.

Take the steak out of the fridge and let it rest half an hour to bring it to room temperature. Peel and slice the garlic into paper-thin slices. Generously season both sides of the steak with salt and pepper. Put 2 Tbsp./25 mL of the butter and the olive oil into a cold cast iron skillet. Place the skillet on the burner and turn the heat to high. Just as the butter is barely melted and starting to sizzle, lay the rosemary sprig and the garlic slices in the pan and place the seasoned steak over top.

Keeping the heat on high, cook the steak for about 3 or 4 minutes on one side until it has a nice brown crust, then turn and cook for another 2 or 3 minutes, just long enough to create a crust on the other side of the steak. Place the skillet in the oven and bake for 10 to 15 minutes or until the center of the steak is 140°F/60°C for medium rare.

Remove the steak from the pan and let it rest on a plate for about 5 minutes. In the meantime, deglaze the pan with the red wine, reducing it by about half. Add the remaining 1 Tbsp./15 mL of butter just at the end, swirling it into the pan sauce. Remove the charred garlic pieces and the rosemary sprig, pour the sauce over the steak and enjoy.

When you're finished the steak, go chop a cord of wood.

flank
STEAK fajitas adobo with Mango Strawberry Salsa

Serves 4

This recipe, which once won me a barbecue in a cooking contest, makes use of the flank steak, one of the tougher and leaner cuts of beef, but also by far the most flavorful. The trick to great flank steak is to make sure you don't overcook it, let it rest before carving and cut thin slices across the grain. This recipe contrasts a spicy marinade with a fruit salsa. It goes well with cold Mexican beer or a light red wine like a Beaujolais.

To marinate the steak

1/2 tsp. | 2 mL kosher salt

1/4 cup | 50 mL lime juice

2 tsp. | 10 mL vegetable oil (flavored oil is best—I like Pecan Chili Oil)

1 Tbsp. | 15 mL ground cumin

1 Tbsp. | 15 mL powdered Ancho or New Mexico chili powder

6 cloves garlic, peeled

2 chipotle chiles in adobo sauce

ground black pepper to taste

1 large flank or skirt steak
(about 1 1/2 to 2 lbs. | 750 g to 1 kg)

For the mango strawberry salsa

2 fresh ripe (but not too ripe) mangos, peeled, pitted and roughly chopped

1/2 cup | 125 mL ripe but firm strawberries, stems removed and roughly chopped

1 jalepeno chili, seeded and finely chopped

A dash or two of Louisiana–style hot sauce

1/2 tsp. | 2 mL kosher salt

1/2 tsp. | 2 mL sugar

2 Tbsp. | 25 mL fresh lime juice

freshly ground pepper to taste

To make the fajitas

12 flour tortillas, wrapped in foil and warmed in a 250°F/120°C oven

1 bunch cilantro, roughly chopped

Blend the salt, lime juice, oil, cumin, chile powder, garlic, chipotles and pepper in a food processor until you have a fairly smooth paste. Place the steak in a nonreactive baking dish and spoon on the marinade, thoroughly coating the steak on both sides. Cover with plastic wrap and refrigerate 6 hours or overnight, turning once or twice.

Half an hour before cooking, combine the salsa ingredients and lightly toss them in a bowl. Season to taste, cover and put in the refrigerator.

Prepare your grill for direct high heat. Place the flank steak on the grill. Turn after 3 minutes and spoon 1 or 2 Tbsp./15 or 25 mL of the marinade on top. Cook for 3 more minutes and flip. Grill for 1 more minute for rare; add a minute or two per side for medium rare. Set the steak on a chopping board, tent with foil and let it rest for at least 5 minutes.

Thinly slice the flank steak across the grain, creating juicy strips of meat, and place in a warmed serving dish. Put out the salsa, cilantro and warmed tortillas. People can now serve themselves, placing a couple slices of meat, then a dollop of salsa, then a sprinkling of cilantro on a tortilla, folding it up and wolfing it down.

grilled Turkey Hill PEPPER STEAK

Serves 4

Turkey Hill Pepper Steak comes to us from gourmand and log home builder John Boys, who got it from someone else who lived in a place called Turkey Hill. I have adapted the recipe, which is usually broiled, for the grill.

1 2-lb. | 1-kg porterhouse steak, 2 to 2¹/₂ inches | 5 to 6 cm thick

kosher salt to taste

1/2 cup | 125 mL whole black peppercorns

1/2 lb. | 250 g butter

1 Tbsp. | 15 mL chopped fresh tarragon

1/2 cup | 125 mL Calvados (French apple brandy)

Take the steak out of the fridge at least an hour before you plan to cook it and pat a fairly generous amount of salt on both sides. Lightly crush the peppercorns in a spice mill or put them in a paper bag and pound them with a flat mallet. Coat the salted steak liberally with the pepper. Let the steak sit until it reaches room temperature, about another ¹/₂ hour.

In a small saucepan gently warm the butter until it is just melted but not sizzling. Add the tarragon and set aside, keeping the butter on the stovetop to keep warm. Preheat your grill for direct high cooking and turn your oven to 200°F/95°C to warm four plates and a serving platter.

Gently warm the Calvados in a small saucepan, being careful not to boil it or expose it to a flame. Keep the Calvados and tarragon butter warm and ready.

Grill the steak for about 3 minutes per side until the peppercorns are throwing off a spicy fragrance. Turn off one side of the grill and cook the steaks over indirect heat for another 3 minutes per side or until the steak is not quite medium rare (internal temperature of about 120°F/50°C). Transfer the steak from the grill to a warmed plate and tent with foil.

When the steak has rested for at least 5 minutes, cut the meat off the bone and slice it into ¹/₂-inch/1-cm strips. Place the steak slices on the warmed platter and bring the platter, the Calvados and tarragon butter to the table. As your guests watch in awe, pour the warmed Calvados over the steak slices and immediately light them with a match. Toss the meat around until the flames subside and then pour the tarragon butter over the steak, tossing again before serving. Be sure you spoon some of the buttery sauce over each serving.

LAMB

Lamb is superb grilled or barbecued. When I was a young man traveling in Europe I had a lamb epiphany during a visit to a Greek youth hostel. One hot afternoon Nicos, the manager, let me help him roast a whole lamb. It was the simplest thing: olive oil, salt, pepper, lemon juice and dried oregano were mixed together in a bowl. The lamb was sewn up with some of this baste inside. The rest of the mixture was painted on the lamb as it slowly rotated on a spit over a pile of charcoal. After about 4 hours the lamb was golden brown and glistening. "Ron, go to the kitchen and get me two Ouzo and cokes and two slices of soft bread," Nicos instructed. I returned with the drinks and the bread and, after a quick glug of the drinks, we ceremonially dragged the slices of bread over the lamb, soaking up the fat and juices. That piece of bread was one of the best things I've ever tasted.

lamb kebabs

Serves 4 as a main course, 6 to 8 as an appetizer

These easy, delicious kebabs make a great party appetizer or a tasty main course. The secret to this dish is to not overcook the lamb, which becomes tough and rubbery if left on the grill too long. Serve either as an appetizer or as a main course on a bed of rice.

To marinate the lamb

1 2-lb. | 1-kg leg of lamb

1/4 cup | 50 mL chopped fresh mint

1/4 cup | 50 mL chopped fresh basil

1 tsp. | 5 mL dried mint

1 tsp. | 5 mL dried basil

1 Tbsp. | 15 mL ground coriander seed

pinch cayenne

1/2 cup | 125 mL extra virgin olive oil

1 tsp. | 5 mL Dijon mustard

zest of 1 lemon, finely chopped

For the kebabs

1 purple onion, cut into bite-sized chunks

16 cherry tomatoes

kosher salt to taste

olive oil, for drizzling

1 lemon (the same one you zested), cut in half for squeezing

Cut the lamb into 1½-inch / 4-cm chunks. Combine all the marinade ingredients and mix thoroughly with the lamb. Place in a resealable plastic bag or a nonreactive bowl, refrigerate and marinate for at least 2 hours, or as long as overnight.

Prepare your grill for direct medium heat. Thread the lamb chunks on 8 long metal skewers or 12 presoaked bamboo skewers, alternating with the onion chunks and cherry tomatoes. Grill the kebabs, turning 2 or 3 times, until the lamb is medium rare (about 6 to 8 minutes), taking care not to overcook it. Remove the skewers from the grill, sprinkle with salt, drizzle with oil and squeeze some lemon juice over them. Serve immediately.

rack of lamb with BALSAMIC REDUCTION

Serves 4 as a main course, 8 as an appetizer

This is a delicious way to grill lamb racks. The balsamic reduction has an incredible sweet tanginess that offsets the earthiness of the dried herbs and brings out the flavor of the meat. Serve as is as an appetizer or as a main course with Rice, Asparagus and Cucumber Salad (page 103).

4 racks of lamb, Frenched by your butcher
(trimmed to bare the ribs and remove the silverskin)

kosher salt to taste

juice of 1 lemon

1/2 cup | 125 mL extra virgin olive oil

2 Tbsp. | 25 mL Dijon mustard

1 Tbsp. | 15 mL chopped fresh rosemary

1/2 tsp. | 2 mL freshly ground black pepper

2 cloves garlic, smashed or pushed through a garlic press

1 cup | 250 mL balsamic vinegar

2 Tbsp. | 25 mL Dijon mustard

1 Tbsp. | 15 mL granulated garlic

1 Tbsp. | 15 mL granulated onion

1/2 tsp. | 2 mL cayenne

1/2 cup | 125 mL Mediterranean Dried Herb Rub (page 54)

1 Tbsp. | 15 mL olive oil

sprigs fresh mint, for garnish

One to two hours before you are going to cook the lamb racks, lightly season the lamb with salt. Combine the lemon juice, 1/2 cup/50 mL oil, 2 Tbsp./25 mL mustard, rosemary, pepper and fresh garlic in a nonreactive baking dish or resealable plastic bag. Add the racks, turning them once or twice to ensure they are evenly exposed to the marinade.

While the lamb is marinating, pour the balsamic vinegar in a small saucepan and bring to a boil over medium-high heat. Cook, watching carefully, until the vinegar has reduced to about 1/2 its original volume (about 10 to 15 minutes). It should be a thick syrup that coats the back of a spoon. Set aside to cool.

Prepare your grill for medium direct heat. Take the lamb out of the marinade, pat the racks dry with paper towels and brush them with the remaining 2 Tbsp./25 mL mustard. Combine the granulated garlic, onion and cayenne and sprinkle lightly over the lamb racks. Coat the racks generously with the herb rub, patting it on with your hands so it sticks to the meat. Drizzle the olive oil over the rubbed racks and pat it into the rub.

Using cherry wood as a flavoring agent, grill the racks for about 4 to 5 minutes per side, or until the internal temperature at the thickest point is about 135 to 140°F/57 to 60°C. To serve, cut the racks into individual chops, arrange on plates and drizzle with the balsamic reduction. Garnish with sprigs of fresh mint.

lamb **meatball** kebabs with MINT JELLY GLAZE

Serves 4 as a main course or 8 as an appetizer

The combination of toasted pine nuts and fresh and dried herbs gives these kebabs a rich flavor and tender but nutty texture. This recipe is a bit fussy because the raw lamb meatballs are very delicate and need to be handled gently when placed on the skewer and when turning on the grill. But man, are they worth the trouble! This is an unbelievably succulent kebab. Serve as an appetizer or a main course with Mimi's Tabouleh (page 106) and some grilled vegetables.

1/2 cup | 125 mL mint jelly

1/4 cup | 50 mL water

1/2 cup | 125 mL pine nuts

1 lb. | 500 g ground lamb

1/2 cup | 125 mL fresh bread crumbs

1 egg, slightly beaten

1/4 cup | 50 mL chopped cilantro

1/4 cup | 50 mL chopped fresh flatleaf parsley

1/4 cup | 50 mL chopped fresh mint

1/2 tsp. | 2 mL dried mint

1 Tbsp. | 15 mL chopped fresh chives

1/2 tsp. | 2 mL dried oregano

1/4 tsp. | 1 mL freshly grated nutmeg

1/2 tsp. | 2 mL kosher salt

generous grinding black pepper

2 or 3 small zucchini, sliced into 3/4-inch | 2-cm disks

10 ripe cherry tomatos

10 smallish button mushrooms or 5 larger ones cut in half

In a small saucepan combine the mint jelly and water and heat, stirring, until the jelly is melted. Set aside.

In a skillet or nonstick sauté pan, toast the pine nuts over medium heat until they turn golden brown. Remove from the pan, cool for a few minutes and coarsely chop the nuts. Combine the ground lamb, pine nuts, bread crumbs, egg, cilantro, parsley, mint, chives, oregano, nutmeg, salt and pepper in a nonreactive bowl.

Wetting your hands to prevent sticking, shape the lamb mixture into about 25 1-inch / 2.5-cm balls. Thread the meatballs onto 5 to 8 soaked bamboo skewers, alternating with zucchini disks, cherry tomatoes and mushrooms. (Press the vegetables gently against the meatballs to help hold them in place while grilling.) At this point you can refrigerate the completed skewers for an hour or two.

Prepare your grill for direct medium heat and oil the grill. Spray the kebabs with cooking spray and place on the grill. Cook for about 4 or 5 minutes per side or until the meatballs are cooked through, brushing with the mint jelly glaze during grilling. (*Note:* these kebabs are touchy. Be careful when you turn them to ensure the meatballs stay on the skewer.)

sexy **MINTY LAMB RACKS** for Two

Serves 2

My friend Arnold Smith says this recipe is one of the sexiest. His wife Yvette calls it an "I want you now" meal, which means when he serves it he usually ends up being dessert.

1/2 cup | 125 mL fresh mint, finely chopped

1/2 cup | 125 mL dark brown sugar

1 Tbsp. | 15 mL white wine vinegar

2 racks of lamb, Frenched by your butcher

Combine the mint, sugar and vinegar, and mix until you have a thick, wet paste, adding a splash more of vinegar if it seems too thick. Coat the lamb racks generously with the paste and grill over medium direct heat for 8 to 12 minutes or until the internal temperature reaches 140°F/60°C for medium rare. Turn every couple of minutes to allow the brown sugar on both sides of the rack to gently caramelize and the flavor of the mint to intensify.

Seafood

Chapter VII

Much as I'd like to think otherwise, man cannot live by meat alone, and nowadays there is an incredible variety of great fish available from all over the world. Most backyard cooks are accustomed to grilling fish, but smoking and planking are rarely used techniques that can really surprise and delight your guests. Here is a range of simple to more complex recipes that will expand your grilling repertoire.

dilled and GRILLED halibut steaks

Serves 4

Halibut is such a delicately flavored fish that you don't want to do much to it. The key here is to use the very freshest ingredients. This dish is excellent with Dilled Lemony Rice (page 94) and your favorite salad.

4 6-oz. | 175-g fresh halibut fillets, skin on

kosher salt and freshly ground black pepper

1/4 cup | 50 mL fresh dill fronds (stems removed), chopped

juice of 1 lemon

extra virgin olive oil

lemon wedges for garnish

Place the fish pieces in a nonreactive dish or baking pan. Season both sides with salt and pepper and coat evenly with the dill. Squeeze lemon over the fish and then drizzle generously with the olive oil to coat. Let sit for 15 minutes. Meanwhile, prepare the grill for direct medium heat.

Place the halibut pieces on the grill, skin side down. Cook for about 6 minutes until just cooked through, to an internal temperature of about 140–150°F/60–65°C. Remove from the grill (the skin will stick to the grill but should easily separate from the fish) and let rest for a couple of minutes. To serve, season with a little more salt and pepper, drizzle with olive oil and accompany with lemon wedges.

pepper-grilled TUNA with wasabi lime mayo

Serves 4

Grilled tuna is one of the most succulent dishes I know. The key here, as with almost all things grilled, is to not overcook. Some like tuna done this way blue-rare, so just the outside of the tuna is seared. I prefer it a little more done, like a medium-rare steak, still translucent in the middle. Serve with Grilled Rice Cakes (page 110).

1/2 cup | 125 mL mayonnaise or aïoli (page 73)

juice of 1 lime

1 tsp. | 5 mL prepared wasabi paste (comes in a tube) or wasabi powder

kosher salt and freshly ground black pepper to taste

2 Tbsp. | 25 mL kosher salt

1 cup | 250 mL freshly cracked black peppercorns

4 8-oz. | 250-g tuna steaks, as fresh as you can get them

olive oil for drizzling

sprigs of cilantro, for garnish

lemon wedges, for garnish

Combine the mayonnaise or aïoli, lime juice and wasabi in a bowl and season with salt and pepper. Make the mayonnaise ahead of time—preferably the night before, but at least an hour before—to give time for the flavors to combine nicely.

Prepare your grill for direct high heat. In a bowl, combine the salt and cracked pepper. Press the tuna steaks into the seasoning mixture until they are well coated on all sides. Drizzle the steaks with olive oil and grill them for 3 to 4 minutes per side. Test for doneness by cutting into a steak with a sharp knife.

Remove the tuna from the grill and place on individual plates and serve surrounded by a drizzle of the wasabi lime mayonnaise and garnished with a sprig or two of cilantro and a lemon wedge.

smoked **OYSTERS**

Serves 4 to 8 as an appetizer

The tinned smoked oysters you can buy at the supermarket taste like oily cardboard compared to these plump, delicious beauties. This is a great thing to do when you've got your smoker up and running for something else. When you've finished your main project, take advantage of the hot smoker and barbecue a few tubs of oysters for later consumption.

1-pint | 500-mL container shucked large fresh oysters (about 8 to 12 oysters)

olive oil

1/4 cup | 50 mL Championship Barbecue Rub (page 51)

kosher salt and freshly ground black pepper to taste

2 Tbsp. | 25 mL butter

1 lemon

Prepare your smoker for barbecuing, bringing the temperature to 200–220°F/95–100°C. Drain the oysters and pat dry with a paper towel. Coat lightly with oil and sprinkle both sides with rub. Let sit for a few minutes until the rub starts to glisten. Spray your cooking grate with vegetable cooking spray and place the oysters on the grate. Smoke for 1 hour, using hickory as the flavoring agent, until the oysters are springy to the touch and have taken on a golden smokey hue. Remove from the smoker.

At this point you can just put them on a serving tray and pass them around, but I like to let them cool and then quickly pan-fry them in butter, finishing them with a sprinkling of salt and pepper and a squeeze of fresh lemon.

grilled SALMON steaks with HOMEMADE BOTTLED SAUCE

Serves 4

One of the best ways to cook salmon is with a soy-sauce-based marinade. I find that the commercial, bottled Asian marinades work very well because they have a thicker consistency than homemade. This sauce uses xanthan gum, a natural thickener, to replicate the silky texture of a bought sauce. The viscosity helps it cling to the fish, giving it a nice shiny appearance and lots of flavor. (Xanthan gum is a white powder available in most health food stores.) This recipe works for swordfish or any strongly flavored, firm-fleshed fish. It goes well with Grilled Rice Cakes (page 110) or Asian Noodle Salad with Sesame Mayonnaise (page 105), and any kind of grilled vegetable.

1 cup | 250 mL light soy sauce

1/2 cup | 125 mL corn syrup

juice of 1/2 lemon (about 2 Tbsp. | 25 mL)

1 Tbsp. | 15 mL white vinegar

1 Tbsp. | 15 mL finely chopped or grated fresh ginger

1 large clove garlic, finely chopped or put through a garlic press

1/2 tsp. | 2 mL xanthan gum

4 6- to 8-oz. | 175- to 250-g fresh salmon steaks or fillets

parsley, for garnish

lemon wedges, for garnish

Combine the soy sauce, corn syrup, lemon juice, vinegar, ginger, garlic and xanthan gum in a small saucepan and bring to a boil over medium heat. Reduce the heat to low and simmer for about 10 minutes. Remove from the heat and cool. (This marinade can be refrigerated for several weeks.)

Place the marinade and the salmon steaks in a resealable plastic bag, squeeze out the air and seal. Marinate for 1 hour.

Prepare your grill for direct medium heat. If you are using hardwood for flavor, go with hickory. Remove the salmon from the marinade and place on the cooking grate. Cook with the cover down for 6 to 8 minutes, or until the salmon springs back to your touch or comes to an internal temperature of about 140 to 150°F/60 to 66°C. Don't overcook! Salmon is best medium rare.

Note that you do not have to turn the fish. In a covered grill it will bake evenly. When ready, the fillets can be lifted right off their skins, which will stick to the grill. Let rest for 3 or 4 minutes and serve garnished with parsley and lemon wedges.

salmon ALJILLO

Serves 4

This is an adaptation of a recipe from a now defunct Toronto restaurant called Iguana.

2 whole dried chipotle chiles

3 whole dried guajillo chiles

4 Tbsp. | 60 mL olive oil

6 large cloves garlic, finely chopped

1 Tbsp. | 15 mL capers

1/4 cup | 50 mL chopped fresh parsley

1/4 cup | 50 mL chopped cilantro

2 tsp. | 10 mL butter

1/2 tsp. | 2 mL kosher salt

juice of 1 lemon

4 6-oz. | 175-g salmon steaks

sea salt and freshly ground black pepper to taste

parsley sprigs, for garnish

Place the chipotle chiles in a bowl of warm water and set aside. Preheat your oven to 375°F/190°C. Place the guajillo chiles on a baking dish and toast them in the hot oven for just 3 or 4 minutes, being careful not to burn them. Remove them from the oven, cut them into pieces with scissors and soak them in a bowl of warm water until soft, about 25 minutes. Purée them until smooth in a blender with 1/4 cup/50 mL of the water they have been soaking in.

Remove the stems and seeds from the softened chipotles and devein them. Cut them into thin strips and set aside.

Heat 2 Tbsp./25 mL of the olive oil in a sauté pan over medium heat and cook the garlic until soft and fragrant, about 5 minutes. Add the chile purée and chipotle strips, capers, parsley, cilantro, butter, salt and half the lemon juice. Cook over medium-high heat until the sauce is bubbling and most of the liquid is evaporated. Remove from the heat and set aside.

Place the salmon steaks on a plate or nonreactive baking dish. Combine the remaining 2 Tbsp./25 mL of the olive oil and the remaining lemon juice and drizzle over the salmon steaks, turning them so both sides are exposed to the mixture. Marinate for 15 to 30 minutes.

Prepare your grill for medium direct heat. Season the salmon with sea salt and pepper. Oil the cooking grate and grill the steaks for about 6 to 8 minutes, depending on the thickness of the steak, until the salmon is just done, using hickory or mesquite as a flavoring agent. Place the salmon on plates, spoon the sauce over top, and garnish with additional parsley.

grilled LITTLE fish

Serves 2 to 4

This technique works with smelts, fresh herring or any other smallish fish like pan-fry-sized trout. Just make sure they are scaled, gutted and ultra fresh. The only thing you need to serve with these is a crisp dry white wine.

1 lb. | 500 g fresh cleaned small fish

kosher salt and freshly ground black pepper to taste

dried oregano (or finely chopped fresh herbs of your choice)

extra virgin olive oil

fresh lemon wedges

finely chopped fresh parsley

Prepare your grill for direct high heat. Pat the cleaned fish dry with a paper towel and place in a nonreactive dish. With a sharp knife cut 3 or 4 diagonal slashes, about 1/8 inch / 3 mm deep, along each side of the fish. Season both sides with salt, pepper and crumbled oregano or chopped fresh herbs. Drizzle with olive oil and pat the herbs and oil into the little slashes with your fingers.

When the grill is hot, place the fish on the grate. Cover and cook for no more than a couple minutes per side. Remove from the heat and season with a little more salt and pepper. Drizzle with some more olive oil and squeeze some lemon juice over the fish. Finish with a sprinkle of the chopped parsley and serve with a lemon wedge and a cold glass of wine.

BARBECUE
≻ SECRETS ≺

One of the problems with grilling fish is the delicate flesh sticks to the cooking grate and the fish seems to fall apart before you can get it off the grill. But today's covered gas or charcoal grills cook so evenly you don't have to turn your fish, even when you're cooking it over direct heat. For fillets, just cook skin side down. The skin sticks to the grill, allowing the fish to come off cleanly and easily. If you're cooking fish steaks that have no skin, be sure you oil the grill and spray the fish with cooking spray just before putting it on the grate.

Extra tip: Don't let that skin go to waste. Salmon skin in particular is excellent when crisped up on the grill. After you've taken your salmon fillet off, pry the skin off the grate and grill it for another few minutes. Remove, sprinkle with salt and it's a crispy and delicious cook's treat!

prosciutto-wrapped **PRAWN** and **LYCHEE** kebabs

Serves 4 as a main course or 12 as an appetizer

This combo might sound strange, but the sweetness of the lychees and the prawns and the saltiness of the prosciutto complement one another very nicely, and the lychee liqueur gives the kebabs a superb aroma. This is ideal as a cocktail party appetizer, but also goes well with rice and a green salad as a main course. (*Note:* wrapping prawns with thin slices of prosciutto is pretty fussy. If you're in a hurry, this dish tastes great even without this embellishment.)

1 20-oz. | 565-g can lychees in syrup

2 oz. | 57 mL Soho lychee liqueur
(mainly used in fancy lychee martinis)

1 tsp. | 5 mL crushed dried chiles

1 shallot, minced

1 Tbsp. | 15 mL finely minced fresh ginger

3/4 cup | 175 mL coconut milk

1/4 cup | 50 mL sunflower oil or other neutral-flavored oil

24 large fresh prawns (13 to 15 to the pound),
peeled and deveined with the tails still on

12 thin slices Italian prosciutto, halved lengthwise

1 Tbsp. | 15 mL cornstarch

1/2 cup | 50 mL cold water

2 Tbsp. | 25 mL fresh mint, finely chopped

limes, for squeezing

Drain the canned lychees, setting aside 12 lychees and 3/4 cup/175 mL of the syrup. Combine the lychees and syrup with the liqueur, dried chiles, shallot, ginger, coconut milk and oil. Toss the prawns in the mixture and marinate for 1 hour at room temperature or 3 hours in the fridge.

Remove the prawns and fruit from the marinade, reserving the liquid. Wrap each prawn with half a slice of the prosciutto, as if you are putting a little belt around the middle of the prawn, taking care that about half of the prawn is still visible. Thread the prociutto-wrapped prawns onto pre-soaked bamboo skewers, placing a lychee after every second prawn. (For cocktail party canapés, thread 1 lychee and two prawns on each skewer.)

Prepare the grill for medium direct heat. While the grill is heating, pour the reserved marinade into a medium saucepan and bring to a slow simmer over medium heat. Mix the cornstarch with the water and pour into the liquid. Bring to a boil and simmer for about 5 minutes or until the sauce is shiny and thick. Set aside.

Oil the cooking grate, place the skewers on the grill, cover and cook for no more than 1 or 2 minutes per side, or until the prawns are barely cooked through. Serve the kebabs drizzled with the sauce and garnished with chopped mint and a squeeze of lime.

hot-smoked SALMON

Serves 6 to 8

When good-quality salmon is barbecued over low heat using hickory, alder, or mesquite smoke as a flavoring agent, the end result is outrageously good. A simple way to barbecue salmon is just to coat a fillet with prepared mustard, sprinkle with Championship Barbecue Rub (page 51), and barbecue for 1½ to 2½ hours, depending on the size and thickness of the fillet. If you want to do something a little fancier, here is my favorite way to barbecue salmon.

1 whole fillet wild salmon (also called a side),
about 1½ to 2 lbs. | 750 to 1 kg

kosher salt and freshly ground black pepper to taste

1 Tbsp. | 15 mL toasted sesame oil

1 tsp. | 5 mL dried red pepper flakes

1/4 cup | 50 mL brown sugar

2 lemons, halved

chopped fresh parsley, for garnish

Prepare your smoker for barbecuing, bringing the temperature to 200–220°F/95–100°C. Put the salmon, skin side down, on a baking sheet or cutting board. With a pair of needle-nose pliers, pluck the pin bones out of the fillet. Season with salt and pepper and coat with sesame oil. Sprinkle the pepper flakes evenly over the fillet and then sprinkle the brown sugar over the top. Squeeze the juice of half the lemon over the sugared salmon. Let the fish sit for 15 minutes or so, until the sugar is wet and glistening.

Place the fillet on the cooking grate, put a chunk or two of hardwood on the coals, and barbecue the salmon for 1½ to 2½ hours, or until the internal temperature at the thickest part reaches about 140°F/60°C. Use two wide spatulas to remove the salmon from the smoker. Transfer to a warmed platter. Garnish with chopped parsley and the remaining lemon, cut into wedges.

smoked **TROUT**

Serves 6 to 8 as an appetizer

Smoked trout is an exotic treat that can be served hot or cold, flaked into a salad, or puréed with seasonings and mayonnaise to make a delicious spread for crackers.

**1 2-lb. | 1-kg whole cleaned trout
(leave the head on if serving it whole)**

1 recipe fish brine (see Smoked Shrimp, page 82)

Soak the fish in the brine for 1 hour at room temperature. Remove from the brine, rinse with fresh water and pat dry. Set the fish on a rack and let it dry for 1/2 to 1 hour, until it develops a glossy skin called a pellicle. (The pellicle helps to hold the juices inside the fish and gives it a lovely appearance when done.) Prepare your smoker for barbecuing, bringing the temperature to 200–220°F/ 95–100°C. Place the fish in the smoker and cook for 1 1/2 hours. Remove from the smoker and serve warm, or cool and serve as a centerpiece for an appetizer platter.

grilled TROUT in foil

Serves 2

The following simple technique gives the fish a more subtle and delicate flavor and texture than grilling over direct heat, and the orange adds a lovely flavor and aroma. Get the freshest possible fish—preferably one you caught in a mountain lake, hours earlier, on a fly rod!

1 whole, cleaned 2-lb. | 1-kg rainbow trout

kosher salt and freshly ground pepper to taste

3 Tbsp. | 45 mL butter, at room temperature

2 Tbsp. | 25 mL chopped fresh parsley

1/2 medium white onion, peeled

2 oranges

sprigs parsley for garnish

Prepare your grill for medium direct heat. Season the trout inside and out with salt and pepper. Tear off a strip of heavy-duty foil 2½ times as long as the fish and double it. Spread 1 Tbsp./15 mL of the butter evenly over the top surface of the foil. Place the fish on the buttered foil. Lightly season the fish inside and out with salt and pepper, and sprinkle with chopped parsley. Slice the onion and one of the oranges into thin rounds and place half of the onion and orange slices inside the body cavity and the other half on top of the fish. Daub the remaining 2 Tbsp./30 mL butter inside the fish and on top of the onion and orange slices. Squeeze half the remaining orange over everything and wrap the foil around the fish, sealing it tightly.

Place on the cooking grate, cover the grill and cook for 8 to 12 minutes or until the fish is just done (about 140 to 150°F/60 to 66°C). You can poke a meat thermometer through the foil in the last few minutes of cooking to check for doneness. To serve, open up the foil, carefully transfer the fish to a warmed platter and pour the juices left in the foil over the fish. Garnish with orange wedges and parsley sprigs.

EVERYONE DESERVES A GOOD PLANKING!

Salmon is central to the traditional aboriginal culture of the Pacific Northwest, and over thousands of years native people developed extremely sophisticated fishing and cooking techniques using the cedar trees that dominate the coastal rainforest. They made fishing line out of cedar bark, boats out of hollowed-out cedar logs, cooking boxes from cedar planks, and they often roasted salmon, fastened to sticks, next to a roaring cedar fire. The flavors of salmon and cedar go so well together that today many west coast restaurants offer cedar-planked salmon on their menus and backyard cooks are learning how to plank. I think planking is the very best way to cook salmon and almost any other kind of seafood, especially firm-fleshed white fish like halibut and sea bass.

Here is the basic planking technique for whole salmon fillets or fish steaks.

1. **Get an untreated cedar or hardwood plank that is ⁵/₈ to 1 inch / 2 to 2.5 cm thick and 8 to 10 inches / 20 to 25 cm wide so it fits easily in your grill.** Most home improvement stores sell plain cedar planks used for fencing for only two or three dollars per plank. Oak, maple or alder planks are not as easily found and are, of course, much more expensive. Most cities have one or two places that sell raw hardwood planks to woodworkers (they also often have hardwood chunks they don't mind selling cheap or giving away). Avoid softwoods like pine and spruce as they impart a bitter flavor.

2. **Presoak the plank in fresh cold water for 6 hours before using.** Bathtubs work pretty well for this, and it doesn't hurt to even soak your planks overnight. WARNING: never use dry planks unless you want a big fire inside your grill! At the very least let planks soak for 1 hour before using.

3. **Marinate or rub your fish ahead of time.** Planking is a fast cooking technique and once you've started the process there's no time to do any prep work.

4. **Preheat your grill for direct high cooking and place the plank, roughest side down, on top of the cooking grate.** In about 3 to 5 minutes it will begin to crackle and smoke, which means it's time to cook your fish. SAFETY NOTE: keep a spray bottle filled with water handy to put out any flames that develop around the edges of the plank, as well as a bucket of water or fire extinguisher just in case things get out of hand.

5. **Place your food on top of the plank and close the cover of the grill.** Cook 3-lb. / 1.5-kg whole sides of salmon or fish fillets that are 1 to 2 inches / 2.5 to 5 cm thick for about 12 to 15 minutes or to an internal temperature of about 140°F / 60°C. No need to turn it over.

This technique bakes the food in the cooking chamber of your grill, surrounded by the aromatic vapors of the smouldering cedar or hardwood plank. When my wife, Kate, tasted her first aromatic, refreshingly astringent bite of cedar-planked salmon she gasped, and said, "This is like having a sauna in your mouth!" The flavor of planked food, particulary seafood, is truly extraordinary. Once you have tried this technique you will want to do it often.

Canadian chef Ted Reader has taken the basic technique of planking to incredible heights, experimenting with woods like oak, mesquite, maple and alder to create otherworldly flavors. I have based the planking recipes in this section on his methods. Run out and buy his book, *The Sticks and Stones Cookbook*, to experience his full repertoire of planking good recipes.

TED READER'S planked SEA BASS WITH CUBAN MOJITO SAUCE

Serves 8

I tried to improve on this superb recipe, but I couldn't, so I'm sharing it with you almost exactly the way I learned it from Ted Reader's book. The Cuban Mojito Sauce should be made in advance.

8 skinless fillets of sea bass
(6 oz. | 175 g each, about 2 inches | 5 cm thick)

kosher salt and freshly ground black pepper to taste

1 recipe Cuban Mojito Sauce (see next page)

2 limes

cilantro sprigs, for garnish

Soak 2 cedar planks for 6 hours and up to overnight. Prepare the Cuban Mojito Sauce and cool.

Season the sea bass fillets with salt and pepper, place in a nonreactive dish and pour half of the sauce over the fish. Let marinate for 30 minutes.

Preheat the grill to high. Season the soaked planks with sea salt, place on the grill, close the lid and bake for 3 to 5 minutes, until they begin to crackle and smoke. Carefully open the lid and place the marinated fish fillets on the planks. (Discard the fish marinade.) Close the lid and bake for 15 to 18 minutes, or until the fish is cooked to medium doneness. Check periodically to make sure the plank is not on fire and use a spray bottle to extinguish any flames. While the sea bass is baking, heat the remaining Cuban Mojito Sauce.

Before removing the fish from the smoker, squeeze the juice of the limes over it. Carefully remove the planks from the grill and, using a metal spatula, transfer the sea bass to a platter. Serve immediately with warm Cuban Mojito Sauce. Garnish with cilantro.

Cuban mojito sauce

Makes approximately 1¹/2 cups | 725 mL

1/4 cup plus 2 Tbsp. | 75 mL vegetable oil

1 medium onion, diced

2 cloves garlic, minced

1 to 2 Scotch bonnet or red jalapeño chiles, seeded and diced

2 roasted red peppers, coarsley chopped

2 Tbsp. | 25 mL chopped cilantro

2 bay leaves

1 cup | 250 mL tomato sauce

kosher salt and freshly ground black pepper to taste

white sugar and fresh lime juice to taste

In a medium saucepan, heat the oil over medium-high heat. Sauté the onion, garlic and chiles for 3 to 4 minutes until tender. Add the roasted red peppers, cilantro and bay leaves and continue to cook for 4 more minutes, stirring occasionally. Add the tomato sauce. Bring the mixture to a rolling boil, reduce the heat and simmer for 15 minutes. Season with salt and pepper. Remove and discard the bay leaves. Purée the mixture, using a hand blender or food processor, until smooth and thick. Adust the seasonings and cool.

Fine-tune the flavorings by adding a pinch or two of white sugar and some squeezes of lime juice.

CEDAR-**planked** salmon **WITH** bourbon-maple glaze

Serves 6 to 8

The sweet, woody flavor of the bourbon and maple glaze complements the richness of the salmon and the aroma of the cedar in this deliciously West Coast dish. Goes well with Rice, Asparagus and Cucumber Salad (page 103).

1 cup | 250 mL real maple syrup

1/2 cup | 125 mL Jack Daniel's Tennessee Whisky

1 tsp. | 5 mL crushed hot red chiles

1 Tbsp. | 15 mL butter at room temperature

1 whole fillet wild Pacific salmon (about 3 lb. | 1.5 kg),
skin on and pin bones removed

kosher salt and freshly ground black pepper to taste

1 tsp. | 5 mL granulated onion

2 lemons

1 Tbsp. | 15 mL finely-chopped fresh flatleaf Italian parsley

parsley sprigs, for garnish

Soak a cedar plank for 6 hours to overnight.

Make the sauce by combining the maple syrup and whisky. Bring the mixture to a low boil and reduce by about half, until you have a thick syrup that coats the back of a spoon. Add the chiles and the butter and stir until just combined. Remove from the heat and set aside, keeping warm on the stovetop.

Prepare your grill for direct high heat. Season the skinless side of the salmon with salt, pepper and granulated onion. Let the salmon sit for 10 or 15 minutes, until the rub is moistened. Season the soaked plank with salt and place it on the hot grill. Close the grill and heat the plank for 3 to 5 minutes, until it is starting to smoke and crackle. Open the lid and place the salmon, skin side down, on the plank. Close the grill and cook for 12 to 15 minutes until the salmon is just cooked through to an internal temperature of 140 to 150°F/60 to 66°C. Check periodically to make sure the plank does not catch fire, and spray the burning edges with water if it does, making sure to close the lid afterwards.

When the salmon is done, squeeze half a lemon along its length and carefully transfer it to a platter. Drizzle half the sauce over the salmon and sprinkle with the chopped parsley. Garnish with parsley sprigs and lemon wedges. Put the rest of the sauce in a serving dish at the table for guests who want extra.

Just Desserts

Chapter VIII

JUST DESSERTS

You'd think that once you've stuffed yourself with barbecue you couldn't even think about dessert, but the opposite is true. A rich meal of barbecued and grilled food simply begs for a satisfying dessert. I am lucky enough to be married to the best dessert cook on earth. My wife, Kate, does not make a huge variety of desserts but when she discovers a great recipe she perfects it. And you, dear reader, are lucky enough to now own the distillation of more than 20 years of home dessert cooking in the Shewchuk household. Read on, cook on, and enjoy.

THE ULTIMATE triple-chocolate BROWNIES

Makes about 12 brownies

This recipe, plus an icing, won a brownie contest about 20 years ago. When these brownies were first served to me by my fellow barbecue team member Kathy Richardier without the icing that was called for in the original recipe, we both agreed that frosting these babies would be overkill *even to us*, which is really saying something. Triple-Chocolate Brownies have been served at least 100 times in my house, and they never fail to provoke ecstatic approval. They freeze superbly, too, although the fact that they are frozen doesn't always keep eager fingers away. *Please note:* the chocolate bars in the brownies should be the big, good-quality European–style chocolate bars. You can probably mess around with the chocolate combination according to your preference, using chocolate bars with hazelnuts or fruit and nut combos, but this basic recipe is so outrageously good you ought to try it as is at least once.

1/2 cup | 125 mL butter

3 oz. | 75 g unsweetened chocolate, chopped

2 eggs, at room temperature

dash salt

1 cup | 250 mL sugar

2 tsp. | 10 mL vanilla extract

1 3-oz. | 75-g bar white chocolate

1 3-oz. | 75-g bar milk chocolate

1 3-oz. | 75-g bar bittersweet or dark chocolate

1/2 cup | 125 mL all-purpose flour

vanilla ice cream, whipped cream or fruit (optional)

Preheat the oven to 325°F/160°C.

Line an 8-inch (2-L) square or round cake tin with foil; grease the inside of the foil generously. Melt the butter in a saucepan over low heat. Remove from the heat and add the unsweetened chocolate. Allow the chocolate to melt completely.

In another bowl, beat the eggs and salt together at high speed for 30 seconds. Gradually add the sugar and keep beating until very thick and pale. Mix in the butter-chocolate mixture and the vanilla. Chop the chocolate bars into pieces and toss them in the flour. Add to the mixture in the bowl and mix well.

Pour into the pan. Bake for about 35 minutes, or until the brownies are firm to the touch.

Serve warm with vanilla ice cream, whipped cream, fruit or nuthin' at all.

mom's chocolate **cake** WITH CHOCOLATE ICING

Serves 8 to 10

Everybody needs a great chocolate cake recipe; this, from an old *Food & Wine* magazine, is the one our family and friends love the most. Kate has messed around with the recipe occasionally, and has found that using milk chocolate instead of dark in both the cake and the icing results in a much sweeter cake that younger kids like. This is a version geared more to grown-ups. Nevertheless, a big glass of milk is the ideal accompaniment. This is best baked the day before serving.

2 cups | 500 mL all-purpose flour

2 tsp. | 10 mL baking powder

2 tsp. | 10 mL baking soda

1 tsp. | 5 mL kosher salt

2 cups | 500 mL sugar

2 cups | 500 mL water

4 oz. | 125 g unsweetened chocolate

6 Tbsp. | 90 mL unsalted butter

1 tsp. | 5 mL vanilla extract

2 eggs, lightly beaten

1 recipe Chocolate Icing (see next page)

Preheat the oven to 350°F/180°C. Butter and flour two 8-inch (1.2-L) round cake pans. Line the bottoms of the pans with wax paper or parchment (don't skip this step or you'll never get this moist cake out).

In a medium bowl, sift together the flour, baking powder, baking soda and salt; set aside.

In a medium saucepan, combine the sugar and water. Bring to a boil over high heat and stir until the sugar dissolves; then pour into a large bowl. Add the chocolate and butter and let sit, stirring occasionally, until the chocolate is melted and the mixture has cooled slightly. Stir in the vanilla.

Beat the eggs into the chocolate mixture at medium speed until combined. Add the dry ingredients all at once and beat at medium speed until smooth. Divide the batter evenly between the prepared pans and bake for about 25 minutes, or until the top springs back when pressed lightly and a cake tester comes out clean. Cool the cakes in their pans for about 25 minutes, then invert onto a rack to cool completely.

Set one cake on a serving platter. Using a metal spatula, spread one-third of the chocolate icing over the cake. Top with the second cake and ice the top and sides with the rest of the icing.

chocolate icing

Makes about 3$\frac{1}{2}$ cups | 875 mL

1$\frac{1}{3}$ cups | 325 mL whipping cream

1$\frac{1}{2}$ cups | 375 mL sugar

6 oz. | 175 g unsweetened chocolate

1/2 cup plus 2 Tbsp. | 150 mL unsalted butter

1$\frac{1}{2}$ tsp. | 7 mL vanilla extract

pinch salt

In a medium saucepan, bring the cream and sugar to a boil over moderately high heat. Reduce the heat to low and simmer, stirring occasionally, until the liquid reduces slightly, about 6 minutes. Pour the mixture into a medium bowl and add the chocolate, butter, vanilla and salt. Let stand, stirring occasionally, until the chocolate and butter have melted.

Set the bowl inside a larger bowl of ice water. Using a hand-held electric mixer, beat the icing on medium speed, scraping the sides occasionally with a rubber spatula, until thick and glossy, about 5 minutes. Use at once.

ginger cake WITH LEMON SAUCE

Serves 10 to 12

The raisins in this are optional, but if you add them and serve the warm cake drizzled with lemon sauce or a dollop of whipped cream, this dessert is Christmas in July. If you don't want Christmas in July, try it warm with vanilla ice cream, instead of the lemon sauce. It's based on the ginger cake from David Lebovitz's *Room for Dessert*, and it tastes like the perfect gingerbread.

1 cup | 250 mL mild molasses

1 cup | 250 mL sugar

1 cup | 250 mL vegetable oil (preferably peanut)

2 1/2 cups | 625 mL flour

1 tsp. | 5 mL ground cinnamon

1 tsp. | 5 mL ground ginger

1/2 tsp. | 2 mL ground cloves

1/2 tsp. | 2 mL black pepper

1 cup | 250 mL water

2 tsp. | 10mL baking soda

1/2 cup | 125 mL fresh ginger, peeled, sliced, and finely chopped

3/4 cup | 175 mL raisins (optional)

2 eggs, at room temperature

1 recipe Lemon Sauce (see next page)

Preheat the oven to 350°F/180°C. Line a 9-inch (1.5-L) round cake pan with a circle of parchment paper. The batter will be runny and may spill, so protect your oven accordingly.

In a bowl, mix together the molasses, sugar and oil. In another bowl, sift the flour, cinnamon, ground ginger, cloves and pepper.

Bring the water to a boil in a saucepan and stir in the baking soda. Pour the contents of the saucepan into the molasses mixture, stirring. Add the fresh ginger.

Add the raisins, if using, to the dry ingredients, then gradually whisk that mixture into the batter. Add the eggs, mixing thoroughly.

Pour the batter into the prepared cake pan and bake for 50 minutes to an hour, or until the top of the cake springs back lightly when pressed or a toothpick inserted into the cake comes out clean. If the top of the cake appears to be browning too quickly, put a piece of foil over it and continue baking until the cake is ready.

Cool the cake in the pan for 30 minutes. Run a knife around the edge of the pan to loosen the parchment paper, then remove the cake and peel off the paper.

Serve with lemon sauce or whipped cream. If you like, you could sprinkle some crystallized ginger in the cream.

lemon sauce

Makes about 1 cup | 250 mL

1/4 to 1/2 cup | 50 to 125 mL sugar

1 Tbsp. | 15 mL cornstarch

1 cup | 250 mL water

2 to 3 Tbsp. | 25 to 45 mL butter

1/2 tsp. | 2 mL grated lemon rind

1$\frac{1}{2}$ Tbsp. | 20 mL lemon juice

1/8 tsp. | .5 mL kosher salt

Combine the sugar, cornstarch and water in the top of a double boiler over boiling water. Stir the mixture together until it has thickened and lost its cornstarch flavor. Remove from the heat and stir in the remaining ingredients. Serve warm.

CLASSIC **lemon meringue** pie

Makes one 9-inch | 23-cm pie

This recipe contains a slight but important adaptation to the classic *Joy of Cooking* lemon meringue pie. Instead of half water, half lemon juice, this recipe calls for undiluted lemon juice for an extra-tangy pie filling.

For the pie

1¹/2 cups | 375 mL sugar

6 Tbsp. | 90 mL cornstarch

1/4 tsp. | 1 mL kosher salt

1 cup | 250 mL fresh-squeezed lemon juice

3 well-beaten egg yolks

2 Tbsp. | 25 mL butter

1¹/2 cups | 375 mL boiling water

zest of 1 lemon, finely chopped

1 baked 9-inch | 23-cm pie shell

For the meringue

4 egg whites, at room temperature

1/2 tsp. | 2 mL cream of tartar

6 Tbsp. | 90 mL white sugar

1/2 tsp. | 2 mL vanilla extract

Combine the sugar, cornstarch and salt in the top of a 2- to 3-quart / 2- to 3-L double boiler over simmering water. Gradually blend in the lemon juice.

When smooth, blend in the egg yolks and butter, stirring constantly. While stirring, gradually add the boiling water, continuing to stir constantly but gently. As the mixture begins to thicken, reduce the heat and stir for another minute. Remove from the heat and stir in the lemon zest. Cool and then pour into the baked pie shell.

Preheat the oven to 325°F / 160°C.

In a deep bowl, whip the egg whites until frothy. Add the cream of tartar and whip the mixture until stiff, but not dry. It should stand in peaks that lean over a little when a beater is removed. Beat in the sugar, 1 Tbsp./ 15 mL at a time, being careful not to overbeat. Gently add the vanilla.

Spread the meringue on the pie, making peaks to your heart's content. Bake for 10 to 15 minutes, until faintly tinged with beige. Remove from the oven and allow to cool completely, then refrigerate. Lemon pie should be served cold, not warm.

blackberry NECTARINE COBBLER

Serves 6

You can use peaches instead of nectarines—or any fruit combination you like. It's nice to have a mix of the tart and the sweet, though, as you do when you mix blackberries with peaches or nectarines. Rhubarb is another great fruit to use in a cobbler.

1 cup | 250 mL sugar

1 Tbsp. | 15 mL cornstarch

3 large nectarines, cut into 1/2-inch | 1-cm pieces
(about 3 cups | 750 mL)

3 cups | 750 mL blackberries

1½ cups | 375 mL all-purpose flour

1½ tsp. | 7 mL baking powder

3/4 tsp. | 4 mL salt

7½ Tbsp. | 110 mL cold, unsalted butter, cut into bits

3/4 cup | 175 mL milk

6 Tbsp. | 90 mL sliced almonds

whipped cream or vanilla ice cream, if desired

Preheat the oven to 400°F/200°C. Butter a 13- x 9-inch (3.5-L) baking dish.

In a bowl, stir together the sugar and cornstarch. Add the fruit and gently combine well. Spread the fruit mixture in the baking dish. In another bowl, whisk together the flour, baking powder and salt. Add the cold butter (if it's not cold, it won't blend properly). Cut the mixture together with a pastry blender or two knives until it resembles coarse meal. Add the milk and stir until just combined.

Drop the dough onto the fruit in mounds, one or two per person. Sprinkle the almonds over the cobbler and bake in the middle of the oven for 20 minutes or until the top is golden. Serve with whipped cream or ice cream.

best BLUEBERRY pie

Serves 6 to 8

This comes from an old *New York Times* recipe, plucked by Kate from the copy machine back when she was a newspaper copy runner in the early 1980s. It's still the best blueberry pie around because it blends fresh, firm berries with cooked, juicy ones. It should definitely be served with the whipped cream; if your friends can't tolerate cream, Cool Whip will do the job.

4 cups | 1 L fresh blueberries

3/4 cup | 175 mL sugar

1/2 cup | 125 mL water

2 Tbsp. | 25 mL cornstarch

4 Tbsp. | 60 mL butter

1/4 cup | 50 mL toasted slivered almonds

1 Tbsp. | 15 mL Cointreau or other orange liqueur

1 baked 9-inch | 23-cm pie shell

1 cup | 250 mL whipping cream

1 to 3 tsp. | 5 to 15 mL granulated sugar, to taste (optional)

1/4 tsp. | 1 mL almond extract

Combine 1 cup / 250 mL of the blueberries, the 3/4 cup / 175 mL sugar and the water in a saucepan over medium-high heat. Bring the mixture to a boil and cook until the berries are soft, about 10 minutes. Cool.

In a separate bowl, mix the cornstarch with a little bit of the juice from the cooled blueberry mixture and stir to dissolve. Add to the saucepan containing the blueberry mixture and cook over medium heat until thickened, stirring so it won't stick to the bottom of the pan. Add the butter and let the mixture cool again.

Stir in the remaining uncooked blueberries, almonds and Cointreau and pour the mixture into the baked pastry shell. Chill.

Before serving, whip the cream, adding the sugar, if desired, and the almond extract. Spoon over the pie or serve on the side.

KATHY'S key lime pie

Serves 8

Unfortunately for my waistline, Kate is not the only person I know who makes great desserts. This recipe, from fellow Butt Shredder Kathy Richardier, is a loose adaptation of a Martha Stewart recipe. Kathy says you can also use the one on the back of the key lime juice bottle when you can find key lime juice.

1³/4 cups | 425 mL graham cracker crumbs

3 Tbsp. | 45 mL sugar

6 Tbsp. | 90 mL butter, melted

pinch salt

1 14-oz. | 398-mL can sweetened condensed milk

5 large egg yolks

3/4 cup | 175 mL key lime juice, or the juice of about 25 key limes
(the fresh juice is wonderfully fresher than bottled, if you can find
the limes and want to bother juicing them)

whipped cream

Preheat the oven to 375°F/190°C. Mix together the graham crumbs, sugar, butter and salt and press into a 9-inch/23-cm pie plate. Bake for about 12 minutes until slightly browned. Cool completely. Reduce the oven temperature to 325°F/160°C.

Whisk the condensed milk, egg yolks and lime juice together. Pour into the cooled crust and return to the oven. Bake until the center is just set, about 15 minutes. Cool completely. Can be chilled in the fridge before serving. Top with whipped cream.

applesauce CAKE with penuche icing

Serves 8 to 10

This spice cake, from the October 1990 issue of *Gourmet* magazine, has a brown sugar frosting that is utterly irresistible. To keep the icing from flowing all over the serving plate, position two pieces of waxed paper, each under half of the cake. After pouring on the icing, wait for it to harden a little, then carefully pull the paper off the platter. You are fully entitled to eat the penuche you find on it. This cake is a marvel when served with cinnamon ice cream.

1/2 cup | 125 mL unsalted butter, softened

1/2 cup | 125 mL sugar

1/2 cup | 125 mL firmly packed light brown sugar

1¾ cups | 425 mL applesauce

1 large egg

2 cups | 500 mL all-purpose flour

2 tsp. | 10 mL baking soda

1 tsp. | 5 mL ground cinnamon

1/2 tsp. | 2 mL freshly grated nutmeg

1/4 tsp. | 1 mL ground cloves

1 tsp. | 5 mL vanilla extract

1/4 cup | 50 mL old-fashioned rolled oats

1 cup | 250 mL raisins, tossed in all-purpose flour to coat them

1 recipe Penuche Icing (see following page)

Preheat the oven to 350°F/180°C. Generously butter two 8-inch (1.2-L) round cake pans.

In a large bowl cream the butter with an electric mixer. Add the sugars gradually, and beat the mixture until it is light and fluffy. Beat in the applesauce and the egg. Sift together the flour, baking soda, cinnamon, nutmeg and cloves, and stir into the mixture until combined. Add the vanilla, rolled oats and coated raisins. Make sure the batter is well combined.

Divide the batter evenly between the two pans. Bake in the middle of the oven for 25 to 30 minutes or until a tester comes out clean. Turn the cakes out onto racks and let them cool completely before icing.

penuche icing

Makes enough icing for a 2-layer cake

3 cups | 750 mL firmly packed brown sugar

3/4 cup | 175 mL unsalted butter

3/4 cup | 175 mL milk

pinch salt

Combine all the ingredients in a heavy saucepan. Bring the mixture to a boil over moderate heat, stirring until the sugar is dissolved. Cook it, undisturbed, until it registers 234°F/112°C on a candy thermometer. Let the mixture cool to room temperature and whisk it until it is thickened, lightened in color, and beginning to lose its sheen.

Working quickly, before the icing has a chance to harden or crystallize, ice the top of the bottom cake, top it with the other layer, and ice the top and sides of the cake. If the icing gets too hard to spread, reheat it over low heat, stirring, until it reaches a spreadable consistency.

grilled PINEAPPLE with caramel sauce

Serves 6

This easy and delicious summer recipe is the perfect end to a grilled dinner. You can also used grilled pineapple slices to top a Asian Chicken Burger (page 114).

1 fresh pineapple

coarsely ground black pepper

**caramel ice cream topping or Mexican cajeta sauce
(available at most Latin specialty stores or gourmet food shops)**

Prepare your grill for direct medium heat. Peel and core the pineapple. Cut into strips 1/2 inch / 1 cm thick and sprinkle them with a little coarsely ground black pepper. Grill the pineapple strips for about 4 minutes per side until slightly charred. Drizzle with warmed sauce and serve.

banana PUDDING

Serves 6 to 8

My Texan friend Amy shared this creamy, sweet and delicious old-school recipe, which she got from her grandma.

3 cups | 750 mL cold milk

1 6-oz. | 150-g box instant vanilla pudding mix

1 8-oz. | 250-g brick Philadelphia cream cheese, softened

1 can Eagle Brand sweetened condensed milk

1 tsp. | 5 mL vanilla extract

1 8-oz. | 250-g container Cool Whip, thawed

5 or 6 sliced ripe bananas

1 7$\frac{1}{4}$-oz. | 200-g box vanilla wafers

In one bowl combine the milk with the vanilla pudding mix. Mix thoroughly and put in the fridge to set.

In another bowl mix the softened cream cheese with the condensed milk. Blend with a mixer until smooth. Stir in the vanilla.

Fold half of the Cool Whip into the pudding mix and then mix in the cream cheese mixture and bananas. Finely crush half the wafers. Line the bowl with wafers, then add a layer of banana slices. Pour half the pudding over this base, then another layer of wafers and bananas (with fewer wafers in this layer), followed by another layer of pudding. Top with the remaining half of the Cool Whip and crumble about 1 cup / 250 mL of wafers to lightly cover the Cool Whip. Garnish with a circle of sliced bananas. Decorate with more vanilla wafers, finely crushed.

rhubarb strawberry COMPOTE

Serves 6 to 8

This recipe comes from my French friend, Michelle Rowan, an excellent cook and translator. If you ever fly in Canada, it's usually Michelle's voice that lectures you in French about the safety procedures on the aircraft. Serve this hot with ice cream or on cheesecake, or serve it cold with whipped cream.

2 cups | 500 mL peeled and diced rhubarb, fresh or frozen

2 cups | 500 mL whole strawberries, fresh or frozen

2 ripe bananas, peeled and cut into 1/2-inch | 1-cm slices

3 Tbsp. | 45 mL sugar (or more to taste)

1 cinnamon stick

Place all the ingredients in a big saucepan. Simmer on low heat for about 30 minutes. Stir frequently.

bourbon and honey **PLANKED** peaches

Serves 8

This delicious recipe is based on the technique of planking god Ted Reader. You can easily substitute ripe pears or nectarines for the peach halves. The key is to use perfectly ripe freestone peaches so it's easy to halve and peel them.

3/4 cup | 175 mL Jack Daniel's Tennessee Whiskey

1/2 cup | 125 mL honey

freshly ground black pepper to taste

freshly grated nutmeg to taste

8 ripe but firm freestone peaches, peeled and halved

1 Tbsp. | 15 mL fresh lemon juice

1 cup | 250 mL whipped cream, sweetened with
a dash of Amaretto, or premium vanilla ice cream

8 sprigs fresh mint

Soak a cedar plank for 6 hours or up to overnight.

In a small saucepan over medium-high heat, combine the bourbon and honey. Season with pepper and nutmeg. Bring to a boil, reduce the heat and simmer until the liquid is reduced by half. Remove from the heat and cool.

Arrange the peaches cut side up in a dish just large enough to hold them in one layer and brush with lemon juice. Spoon 1 Tbsp./15 mL bourbon-honey mixture over each peach and let marinate for 1 hour.

Preheat the grill to high. Place the soaked plank on the grill, close the lid and bake for 3 to 5 minutes or until it begins to crackle and smoke. Carefully lift the lid, place the peaches on the plank, cut side up, and close the lid. Cook for 3 to 5 minutes or until the peaches are hot and tender, and starting to char on the edges. Remove from the plank and transfer to dessert plates. Garnish each with a dollop of whipped cream or ice cream, drizzle with the remaining bourbon-honey mixture, add a sprig of mint and serve immediately.

What to Drink and Listen to with Your Barbecue

Chapter IX

WHAT DO YOU SERVE WITH BARBECUE?

During competition, cold beer goes down great—and if you pace yourself you don't get too hammered by judging time. We also have a tradition of martinis at dawn...or was that shots of tequila at dawn? For some reason the memory is fuzzy. Generally I like to serve beer and wine to accompany grilled or barbecued food. Dry, hoppy beers go nicely with richer barbecue, as do fruity, spicy white wines like Gewürtztraminer and crisp, citrusy Sauvignon Blancs. And, of course, there's nothing like a big chewy red to go with steak or lamb. The key is to maximize your eating and drinking pleasure, and one way to turn up the fun volume is to start off the party with a nice cocktail. Here are a few of my favorites.

CUBA LIBRE serves 1

Have one of these and it's summer...even if it's twenty below zero.

1½ oz. best quality white rum

1/4 fresh lime

cold Coca-Cola

Fill a highball glass with ice cubes, pour in the rum, squeeze in the lime juice, top up with Coke.

PIMM'S CUP #1 AND GINGER serves 1

These sneaky little cocktails are innocuous enough, until your face starts to feel as if it's made of rubber.

1½ oz. Pimm's Cup #1 liqueur

cold ginger ale

1 orange slice

Fill a highball glass with ice, pour in the liqueur, top with ginger ale and garnish with an orange slice.

WILD MUSTANG serves 1

Any more than one of these and I cannot guarantee you will be able to control your feelings.

1½ oz. chilled vodka

4 oz. chilled champagne

Combine and serve in a chilled champagne or martini glass.

KIR serves 1

Hand one of these to your guests as they arrive and suddenly it's a special occasion.

1/2 oz. crème de cassis

4 oz. crisp dry white wine
(white Burgundy Aligoté is the classic)

Pour the crème de cassis into a white wine glass. Gently pour the wine over top, taking care not to mix them too much. The drink should look like a clear version of a Tequila Sunrise, with the heavier Cassis lurking at the bottom. (For extra-special Kir Royale, subsitute chilled Champagne for the white wine.)

ROCKY MOUNTAIN MARGARITAS

One batch makes 2 blenders of margaritas, enough for 8 to 12 drinks

I call these Rocky Mountain Margaritas because the blue curaçao combined with the green limeade concentrate gives the drinks an emerald glow like a glacier-fed river or a high mountain lake.

2 fresh limes, cut into wedges

kosher salt

1 12-oz. | 350-mL container limeade concentrate, thawed

1 cup | 250 mL water

1 8 1/2-oz. | 235-mL bottle lime juice from concentrate

10 oz. tequila

6 oz. blue curaçao (or Triple Sec)

Pour 2 Tbsp./25 mL of coarse salt onto a small plate. Wet the rims of 4 large margarita glasses with a wedge of lime and dip the rims into the salt. Set aside. Combine the thawed limeade concentrate, water, lime juice, tequila and blue curaçao in a jug or large measuring cup. Fill a blender with ice cubes. Pour in the mixture to cover the ice cubes and whiz until it has the consistency of a Slurpee. Fill the glasses and go for it!

CAMPARI COCKTAIL serves 1

Pretentious? *Mais oui.* But delicious? *Bien sur.*

1 measure Campari

freshly squeezed juice of 1 orange

Perrier or soda water

lemon or lime slice

Fill a short, wide (old fashioned) glass with ice cubes and add the Campari, juice and Perrier or soda water. Mix and decorate with a slice of lemon or lime.

ACK-ACK-A-DAQ!

This, my friends, is the ultimate summer blender drink. It should only be made when local peaches are at the peak of their ripeness, the sky is deep blue and the ambient temperature is over 90°F / 32°C. This is the kind of drink that should be hand-delivered to your beautiful wife as she reads a trashy novel in a chaise longue wearing a cheap straw hat. One of these and she will love you forever. Two of them and she will love you as soon as she's finished the drink.

1 Tbsp. sugar

ice cubes

3 or 4 ripe fresh peaches, peeled, pitted and cut into chunks

5 oz. white rum

1 1/2 oz. peach schnapps

chilled soda water

sugar to taste

fresh lime juice to taste

Rim four wide-mouthed glasses with sugar and set aside. Fill a blender about half full with ice cubes. Place peach chunks on top of the ice. Pour rum and schnapps in, then top up to cover the ice and peaches with the soda water. Whiz until smooth and frothy. Jack up the flavor with a little sugar and some fresh lime juice (especially important if the peaches aren't quite ripe). Pour into the glasses and serve immediately.

MUSIC TO BARBECUE BY

Remember, barbecue is not just a food, it's a lifestyle, and a lifestyle needs a soundtrack. There have been many songs written about barbecue and even some CD compilations of barbecue music, but I think the place to start is asking yourself the question, "What music do you most associate with the good life—great food, best friends, summer fun?" Whatever the answer is, that is what you should throw into the CD player when you are cooking up some barbecue. Of course, classic blues and country music go naturally with barbecue, but so do jazz, rock 'n' roll and world music. After many years of intensive, liver-damaging research, here are my top 10 CDs to barbecue by. There are many CDs out there with great songs on them, but all of these are truly great, soul-healing albums that are able to withstand many playings over time.

10. *Avalon Sunset*, Van Morrison

9. *Live at Blues Alley*, Eva Cassidy

8. *Blood on the Tracks*, Bob Dylan

7. *Clandestino*, Manu Chao

6. *Trampoline*, The Mavericks

5. *A Collection of Hits*, Kathy Mattea

4. *Legend*, Bob Marley and the Wailers

3. *The Mountain*, Steve Earle and the Del McCoury Band

2. *Car Wheels on a Gravel Road*, Lucinda Williams

1. *The Essential Waylon Jennings*, Waylon Jennings

Thanks to CD-burning technology, with the help of a computer and a CD burner you can make your own custom barbecue CD—and with online music services like Apple's iTunes, you can grab songs for a few cents apiece. Here's my ultimate barbecue mix—a bit of a hodgepodge, but I guarantee if you burn this list on to a CD you will be a step closer to Barbecue Nirvana.

Track 1:   *Seminole Wind*, John Anderson

Track 2:   *Sweet is the Melody*, Iris Dement

Track 3:   *You're a Big Girl*, Bob Dylan

Track 4:   *Walking in Memphis*, Marc Cohn

Track 5:   *Uncle John's Band*, Grateful Dead

Track 6:   *A Song for You*, Gram Parsons

Track 7:   *I'd Rather Go Blind*, Etta James

Track 8:   *Hound Dog*, Big Mamma Thornton

Track 9:   *Burnin' Love*, Elvis Presley

Track 10: *Sweet Home Alabama*, Lynyrd Skynyrd

Track 11: *La Grange*, ZZ Top

Track 12: *Takin' Care of Business*, BTO

Track 13: *Curtis Mayfield*, Superfly

Track 14: *Jamming*, Bob Marley and the Wailers

Track 15: *Take Me to the River*, Al Green

Track 16: *Dream in Blue*, Los Lobos

Track 17: *Rocket*, Kathy Mattea

Track 18: *It's a Great Day to be Alive*, Travis Tritt

Track 19: *Windfall*, Son Volt

All I ever needed to know, I learned from barbecue

with apologies to Robert Fulghum

Most of what I really need to know about how to live, and what to do, and how to be, I learned from cooking barbecue. Wisdom is not at the top of the culinary school mountain, but there on the grill and in the barbecue pit.

These are the things I learned. Put mustard and rub on everything. Don't use MSG. Don't start your coals with chemicals. Barbecue downwind from your neighbors. Oil your grill before you put your meat on. Don't take credit for recipes that aren't yours. Say you are sorry when you undercook the ribs. Wash your hands before you carve the brisket. Drink heavily. Coleslaw and beans are good for you. Strike a balance between work, family and barbecue. Cook some and eat some and drink some and laugh and sing and dance and play and use your grill or smoker every day.

Take a nap between spraying and turning your pork butt. When you prepare your meat for the judges, use fresh lettuce, present six portions, and go easy on the sauce. Be aware of the internal temperature. Remember the dipping sauce in the little plastic cup? The meat goes in and gets eaten and nobody really knows how or why. Barbecue is like that.

And then remember that book about Barbecue Secrets and the first meat you ever barbecued, and the most flavorful hardwood of all: HICKORY! Everything you need to know about barbecue is there somewhere. Slow and low and smoke and sweet, salty, sour, bitter, and hot, fat and protein and the beauty of perfectly cooked meat.

Think of what a better world it would be if we all, the whole world, had barbecue and peach daiquiris about 3 o'clock every afternoon and then lay down for a nap with a bag of charcoal for a pillow. Or we had a basic policy in our nation and other nations to always cook great barbecue and scrape the grill when we're done. And it is still true, no matter how old you are, that when you go to a barbecue contest it is best not to eat beforehand.

ACKNOWLEDGEMENTS

This book has been a long time coming and I have many people to thank for helping bring it into the world.

My barbecue team, the Butt Shredders past and present—Rocco Ciancio, Kathy Richardier, Amo Jackson, Ian Baird, Tom Masterson, Stephen Robertson, Heather Rooke, Kenny Stef, Vince Gogolek and Dave Thurgar—are more than my team mates on the competitive circuit. They are my friends and fellow adventurers on a journey of discovery that has led us all to bold new worlds of barbecue. You guys are the greatest!

Gail Norton, a good friend, a true food visionary and the doyenne of the Calgary culinary scene, asked me to teach my first cooking class many years ago and has supported me year after year. Thanks, Gail!

This book contains pretty much everything I know, which isn't a lot. Barbecue Secrets would be a lot slimmer if not for the generous contributions of Butt Shredders Kathy, Ian, and Vince as well as my brother Allan Shewchuk, Gail Norton, Amy Walker and her mom Nadine Ryan, Arnold Smith, Margie Gibb, Stuart Parker and Michele Allaire, Rob Glaser and Judith Cartwright.

For me this has been as much a creative writing project as a cookbook. Barbecue Secrets would not read nearly as well as it does without the editorial advice and support of Stephen Cole, David Murray, Jim Dingwall, Rick McCharles and Zsuzsi Gartner. Thanks for looking at the drafts and helping me smooth out the rough edges!

The photography in this book is spectacular. Photographer John Sinal, food stylist Joanne Facchin and Whitecap art director Roberta Batchelor joined forces in one crazy weekend to create 16 of the best barbecue photographs ever. And we could not have pulled off the two-day photo shoot without the generous hospitality of Paula and John Masterson, who opened their spacious and beautiful home to us and turned what could have been an ordeal into a pleasure. The food photos are complemented by lots of informal shots scattered throughout this book. They were taken at barbecue events by Rick McCharles, Ian Baird, Peter Findlay and Vince Gogolek, to whom I am grateful.

Thanks also to my agent Robert Mackwood, who represents me far better than I ever could and who is a storehouse of sage wisdom and expert advice.

And of course this book would not exist without the fabulous team at Whitecap Books—Michael Burch, Robert McCullough, Robin Rivers, Elaine Jones, Jacqui Thomas, Roberta Batchelor, Janice Ackroyd, Susan Adamson, Sandra Kevac, Sophie Hunter and Monica Bisal—whose combined talents make for one of the great publishing houses in Canada.

I cannot forget to thank North America's barbecue pioneers, starting with Chef Paul Kirk, the Baron of Barbecue. Paul is the first true barbecue champion to openly share his winning barbecue style. Thousands of people all over the world, including yours truly, have benefited from his sound techniques and delicious recipes. Thanks also to Bob Lyon, the Grandfather of Barbecue in the Pacific Northwest, who has been a tireless promoter of competitive barbecue and a huge supporter of the Canadian barbecue scene. A posthumous thanks to the late, great Fire Chef, David Valjacic, who was the first to bring championship barbecue to Canada, and Carol and Sandy Dougall, longtime barbecue aficionados who learned what David was doing in Vancouver and brought a great barbecue contest, Barbecue on the Bow, to Calgary in 1993, where it has thrived ever since.

Finally, and most importantly, I would like to thank Canada's greatest barbecue widow, my loving yet sarcastic wife, Kate. Not only has she put up with ten years of summer weekends that were devoted to barbecue instead of household chores, she is also a brilliant writer and editor whose insights—and great dessert recipes—have made a huge contribution to this book.

INDEX